Tea & Sympathy 🫖

Tea & Sympathy

◆ The Life of an English Teashop in New York ◆

Anita Naughton with 60 Recipes and an Introduction by Nicola Perry

G. P. PUTNAM'S SONS

New York

A list of photo and art credits appears on page 195.

G. P. Putnam's Sons
Publishers Since 1838
a member of
Penguin Putnam Inc.
375 Hudson Street
New York, NY 10014

Library of Congress Cataloging-in-Publication Data

Naughton, Anita, date.
Tea & Sympathy : the life of an English teashop in New York / Anita Naughton.
p.   cm.
ISBN 0-399-14937-6
1. Tea & Sympathy (Teashop)—History.   2. Cookery.   I. Title.
TX945.5.T43 N38   2002   2002068366
641.5—dc21

Printed in the United States of America
1   3   5   7   9   10   8   6   4   2

This book is printed on acid-free paper. ∞

BOOK DESIGN BY AMANDA DEWEY

For Noel, Dominique, and Marlon. And for my mother, who loved and believed in me.

—*Anita Naughton*

♦ ♦ ♦

To my parents, Mr. Ted Perry, M.B.E., and Mrs. Doreen Perry/Cole, for making it all possible and believing in me, and to my fantastic husband, who is my calm in the storm that is my life.

—*Nicola Perry*

Acknowledgments

Anita Naughton wishes to thank: my brother Phil, for always being available to advise and help; Suzanne McConnell, for the years of support and friendship, the writing class and its students; Gary Kuehn, for the kick in the pants; the Writers Room, for providing sanctuary and friendships; Amy Seeham and JoAnna Beckson, for putting me on track; Fiddlesticks; Estelle Lazarus; John Ryan; my family: Dad and Danielle, Patrick, Dominic, Geddy, Michael & Daisy; and Marie and Bob Weltzien. Special thanks go to my friends Janine, Melly, Bastianne, Cara, Jen, Yutta, Mark d'Inverno, Pennel Bird, Rob Galinsky, Rick Hemmings, Philippe Cheng, and to Don Perlis, for his friendship and wallet. Thanks to Errin Aries, for loan of breast pump; Fara Krasnopolsky, for inspiration; Robert, Red, and all the Tea & Sympathy regulars.

My aunt Mimi Merzeau, Thérèse and Pierre Langé, Françoise Gaillard, Genevieve Broquet and Luz Garraud, and my sister-in-law, Marlisa, for babysitting.

I am especially grateful to my agent, Claudia Cross; my editor, Hillery Borton, who made it all possible; and Penguin Putnam.

My love and thanks to Nicky Perry and my wonderful friends from Tea & Sympathy, in the kitchen and out, for all their love and encouragement, and personalities, without which I could never have written this book.

Nicola Perry would like to thank: All of the people who made this book possible. To all the people who have worked at Tea & Sympathy over the years, many of whom are still with me. I can't begin to explain how important all the staff at Tea & Sympathy are to me. They have been my friends, confidants, sources of amusement, touchstones with reality and above all the lifeblood of the restaurant. From dishwashers to waitresses they have been ambassadors of the truth and the constants that make up the backbone of day-to-day business.

The other people I have to thank are of course the patrons of Tea & Sympathy, some friends who became customers and some customers who became friends. All of them have taught me about the way different people make up the world.

I should also take this opportunity to thank the people I worked with, and for, in restaurants in both New York and London. These people taught me how to deal with people, and in some instances how not to.

I would be wrong not to thank everyone who worked with me on this book: Claudia Cross, my literary agent, who had the conviction to see that our publisher would make this book what it should be. To Hillery Borton, our editor at Penguin Putnam, who had the understanding of what Tea & Sympathy was all about and was able to guide the process of creating a book that would be a true expression of the living entity that it is today. Thank you to all the wonderful photographers who captured the images in the book, which have served as proof of so many of our amazing moments.

On a more personal note, I have to thank my parents, who always believed in me and not only gave me life but also gave me the money to start the real Tea & Sympathy that I had dreamed of since I was twenty-three.

One last thank-you, to Tea & Sympathy itself, without which I would never have met my beloved husband, Sean Kavanagh-Dowsett.

Contents

Introduction

Strangers show a real interest when I mention I have a restaurant, but when I tell them it's British they blanch and make excuses. "Come on give it a try," I say. They do, and invariably these skeptics end up becoming my regular customers.

Most people think of "British cuisine" as an oxymoron despite the fact that Britain has a long cooking tradition. The problem is that until quite recently, we Brits, unlike the French, had no true restaurant culture. Dining out could be a nightmare. One was better off eating at the local pubs, which offered basic, traditional fare.

At home we've always enjoyed an endless variety of delicious and inventive traditional foods. Take a walk in England on a Sunday afternoon, and all the streets brim with the pungent aroma of the Sunday roast, sizzling in the oven with all its trimmings: crispy parsnips, roast potatoes and golden Yorkshire puddings soaked in gravy. More than likely there'll be bowls of apple and blackberry crumble drenched in hot vanilla custard to follow. There's the wonderful tradition of pie making, both sweet and savoury, as well as the legendary English breakfast: a tasty fry-up guaranteed to cure a heavy night at the pub. And of course the ultimate British institution, afternoon tea: Served between four and five o'clock, cups of steaming fragrant tea accompany tasty finger sandwiches, delicious cakes and scones piled high with Devonshire clotted cream and strawberry jam.

Nicky paints a bench.

When I first arrived in New York I couldn't find any of these familiar dishes, or if I did they were poor imitations. One freezing cold evening, while we were standing on Fifth Avenue trying desperately to hail a cab, Kate Pierson, singer for the B-52's, turned to me and said, "Do you know what, Nicky? There's no place here to get a decent cup of tea."

That was it, something clicked inside me. I decided then and there that I wanted my own restaurant. I even knew what I wanted. It would be a cross between a British café, a teashop, and an English restaurant with a pub atmosphere. Most important, a place where you could sit and gossip over a proper cup of Rosie Lee (that's Britspeak for a *cuppa tea*).

The world-renowned Dame Barbara Cartland, romance novelist and stepmother to Princess Diana. We made her a Victoria sandwich birthday cake, and Nicky's friend Margaret Braun, the well-known wedding-cake maker, kindly decorated it for us.

In my childhood the kettle was constantly on the boil, so that a cup of tea could be had at any time of the day. In England, tea is enjoyed by all classes and on all occasions. Whether you've lost your job, won the jackpot, found your wife in the arms of your best mate, you'll invariably hear the comforting refrain "Sit down luv and have a cuppa." Tea is the great consoler—even the Queen never travels anywhere without her kettle and boils only bottled English springwater for her tea.

I spent the next ten years working in a variety of restaurants—some of them fast-food joints, some of them the best restaurants in New York. I learned a lot and met a lot of people. I was a poor waitress desperate to buy my own tables, so to speak.

In an act of divine intervention, I was knocked off my bicycle and spent the next four months laid up with an excruciating knee injury. When I did at last return to work I knew it was time to hang up my pinny and give myself a promotion. The question now was finding a place.

Five years earlier I'd worked for a caterer on Jane Street. Every night on my way home I used to peer through the windows of the Greenwich Time café and think *God this would make a perfect little teashop!* As it turned out, when I asked the vegetable delivery man if he knew of any restaurants up for grabs, he told me that Greenwich Time was vacant. Within six weeks I had signed the lease and Tea & Sympathy finally came into being.

Things have moved on since we first opened shop, but I always impress on my girls just how much we depended on our early regulars. They kept us going before the place really took off.

One eminent journalist referred to the teashop as a "colonial outpost." It's an apt description, especially when I

David Bowie at his fiftieth birthday party at the restaurant, which was filmed for British television. One of the rare days that we closed to the public.

think that David Bowie chose to spend his fiftieth birthday giving interviews from T&S and Dame Barbara Cartland requested one of my Victoria Sponge Sandwich Cakes for her ninetieth birthday.

♦ ♦ ♦

One of the valuable lessons I learned in cooking is that most recipes are only guidelines to which one can add or omit ingredients depending on taste. For instance, I've made the soups vegetarian and dairy free, but if you prefer, the lentil soup can be enhanced with a

Former waitress and current artist Cathy Yarrow looks on as Nicki strikes a pose.

ham bone, and the rich green of the watercress soup paled with a dash of heavy cream. But most of us need these basic guidelines before we can turn our own creativity loose.

The recipes in this book are simple to follow and can be used by experts and novices alike. Best of all, the ingredients can easily be found at your local market. The advantage of this cookbook is that all the dishes are served in the restaurant and so they've been tested and approved by thousands of my customers.

For all the customers over the years who've wanted recipes, here you have it— the *Tea & Sympathy* cookbook.

—*Nicola Perry*

About Tea

I am often asked which tea should go with which foods. The obvious answer is subtle teas with milder foods and more robust teas with stronger tasting foods. Tea is like wine in this respect and in the fact that most teas we think we are familiar with are actually blends of many teas combined to achieve a desired flavour, with allowances for the variables of seasonal aberrations as well as economic fluctuations. As many as thirty teas can be blended to make your average supermarket brand, and these blends as well as those of the high-end teahouses are closely guarded secrets.

In the rather rarified atmosphere of the tea glitterati, they have their own vocabulary and very specific ways of making tea, but unless you want to ruminate over "the biscuity" quality of the brew you just spat out almost exactly five minutes and thirty seconds after "the agony of the leaves," I think it is better to know the basic characteristics of teas and try the ones that sound best to you. Don't be afraid to combine different teas to make your own blend. Tea should be enjoyed the way you like it and is just as appropriate in the guise of a quick cuppa as it is when drunk from fine bone china as long as the tea is prepared correctly, allowing the tea to infuse the brew with all the accompanying flavour and smells.

Here are a few tea facts for you to know, not just names, but also types of teas, and even some non-teas, but that should become clear below. Armed with a bit of basic knowledge you can venture forth into the world of the tea drinker and possibly do yourself some good too.

Types of Tea

When it comes to teas, there are three categories: black, oolong and green. These refer to the way the leaves are prepared.

BLACK TEA   This type of tea is the most popular in America. The leaves are crushed and then oxidised before being dried.

OOLONG   These teas are only partially oxidised, and then they are pan fried. This crucially timed blast of heat and moisture arrests the oxidation process, leaving the tea a lighter green-brown. The partial oxidation generally makes for a more delicate-tasting tea.

GREEN TEA   So called because these teas are processed and dried without being allowed to oxidise. These delicate teas are highly regarded for their healthful properties.

Beyond these basic three categories, I should mention two exceptions.

WHITE TEA   These are very rare and correspondingly very expensive. Their delicate taste makes them a real connoisseur's tea; you would not want to blend them with another tea, as their characteristics would be lost.

HERBAL TEAS   More correctly referred to as *tisanes*. These teas are in a category of their own because they do not contain any tea. This is a general category for dried preparations to which boiling water is added and a brew produced in the same manner as a tea.

This group is made up of dried fruits and/or herbs and spices, such as mint and chamomile. As result, they tend not to have any caffeine content (except yerba maté, a traditional Argentinean tea that has a very high caffeine content). These should not be confused with flavoured teas, which generally have a black tea base.

Here are some specifics on the subdivisions within these groups of tea.

ASSAM   This is a rich, full-bodied pungent tea that is a perfect all-occasion drinking tea. It is grown in the Assam region of northeastern India, where it was discovered growing wild in the 1830s by the Scotsman Robert Bruce. Prior to his discovery, all teas came to the West from China.

CEYLON   This category includes any black or green teas grown in Sri Lanka, which vary in quality. The finest varieties are grown at higher elevations and have a full flavour and fragrance that make this another tea that is excellent to drink anytime.

DARJEELING   Grown in the high Himalayan foothills of India, this black tea is considered one of the worlds finest, and accordingly a fine quality example can be quite expensive. The delicate flavour is among the most subtle of the black teas, and connoisseurs describe it as having a hint of black currant.

EARL GREY   This flavoured black tea originally from China is said to have been brought back to England by the Second Earl Grey in the 1830s. It is actually a blend of black teas that are flavored with oil of bergamot, an Italian citrus fruit. This is an ideal afternoon tea, which can be served with or without milk or sugar to taste.

ENGLISH BREAKFAST   A blend of Assam and Ceylon tea. As its name implies, it is a perfect tea for mornings, and its full, well-rounded flavour stands up well to bold foods, like the classic British fried breakfast.

JASMINE   This tea, which can be either all green or pouchong tea, is flavoured with jasmine. This combination of a delicate tea base with the fresh aroma of jasmine petals makes this tea ideal for afternoon tea. Whenever I have jasmine tea, the wonderful aroma reminds me of the delicate perfume of night-scented jasmine on a warm summer evening.

LAPSANG SOUCHONG   This black Chinese tea has a very distinctive smokey taste and aroma. The "souchong" refers to the leaf size, meaning the third leaf down from the top of the plant. Some people find the smokiness a little bit of an acquired taste, but I think it is a very elegant tea that is better sipped and enjoyed rather than gulped from a mug.

◆ ◆ ◆

When looking for tea without caffeine you can either choose an herbal tea (not a tea after all) or opt for a decaffeinated tea. Remember, no method of decaffeination removes all of the caffeine, but it can remove upwards of 90 percent. When considering caffeine in tea you should remember that tea has an effect very different from that of coffee. With tea, caffeine enters the system gradually as opposed to the spiky jolt that coffee delivers.

A Cuppa Rosie Lee

Select a tea of your liking. Swirl boiling water in the teapot and then empty it out. This will warm the pot so proper brewing can take place. If you are using loose tea you can add one teaspoonful of tea for each person plus one for the pot. Bring fresh water to a rolling boil and pour it directly into the teapot.

The teapot must now be left so that the tea can "steep." About five minutes is a good amount of time for the hot water to extract the full flavour of the tea. Small-leaved teas, like a green tea, will take less time.

Give the teapot a stir and then get ready to serve. If you are using loose tea you will need to place a strainer between the spout and the cup.

It is customary to pour the milk into the teacup first. This tradition, which dates back to the era when delicate China cups were used, was observed by those who wished to avoid cracking the cups by pouring hot tea into them. If you were very rich, the tea was poured in first, to show that you could afford to replace your broken teacups. Nowadays we tend to put milk in last to control the colour of the tea.

When using a tea bag in a cup, it is best if you warm the cup first with boiling water. If you are making a pot of tea with tea bags, then the rule is one tea bag per every two or three cups.

Prologue:
The Last Shift

In the last hour of my final shift at Tea & Sympathy I begin to see everything from a new perspective. I am lying on my back between the Welsh dresser and the cake counter, my head near the cappuccino machine, my feet pointing due south down Greenwich Avenue.

My future husband interrupts his work every few moments to make reassuring noises though the kitchen hatch. My boss, Nicky, is making frantic phone calls to the other waitresses. "How can you let her work, you heartless cow? She's eight months pregnant!" she shouts into their answering machines. "If she gives birth today, I'll blame you!"

I should be a nervous wreck too, but I am feeling oddly relaxed. The truth is, it is my fault I'm lying here: I'd wanted to work for as long as possible; I'd carried on as if nothing was happening to my body. This final day I'd left behind a trail of devastation and spilt gravy as I bumped between the ten tables of the tiny little English teashop and restaurant.

Then I took one last order from table number six—"an extra side of bacon, well done"—and the nausea hit me.

I made it behind the counter and collapsed out of view of the customers—although if anyone had been sitting on table one he or she would have seen me up to my knees. I'd often sat on that table over the years and written in my journal, little scraps and stories from my life in New York.

It strikes me as I lie here that after nearly a decade at Tea & Sympathy I've never really noticed the ceiling before. It's a pressed-tin ceiling in British racing green, with a permanent dip just above the tea caddies. I can remember this happening when the woman who lived in the apartment above accidentally left her bath water running; Nicky had to break into the apartment to turn the tap off.

Lying there, I listen to Nicky's movement around the restaurant. She always helps us on a Sunday anyway, so she knows the idiosyncrasies of certain regulars: that table ten likes raspberry preserves with his toast and a little jug of thick cream for his tea or that the poet on table nine likes her tea made half and half with Assam and Ceylon. Fortunately most of the customers have been served. I can lie here in relative peace until someone orders tea and I'll have to move away from the hot-water nozzle.

I know that it's my last day, and I feel like a condemned woman. My life seems to flash before my eyes, and I just want to savour every last sensation.

I suppose it needed something this extreme to make me finally quit. The fun's over; now get on with life, I tell myself. But in my mind's eye, all I can see is a younger me running along Greenwich Avenue so as not to be late for her shift.

CHAPTER ONE

Sunday Morning
in the Village

I t's Sunday morning, and I have a hangover. As I walk through the door, Big Jimmy says, "You look like shit."

"Do I?" I reply, forcing a smile.

You've got to be careful with old Jimmy; he's quick to take offense. Last Sunday, I happened to call him an "ugly bastard" and, just as the morning reached its busiest, he put all the breakfast orders out at the same time. Then he kept on ringing the kitchen bell. It was a terrifying experience. I had to go through all the checks trying to match them with the breakfast plates on the hatch: scrambled eggs (with an extra rasher of bacon), scrambled eggs (with a Cumberland instead of a banger), tomatoes (on seven-grain toast), tomatoes (on white toast), porridge (with nuts and raisins), porridge (with nuts, raisins, and bananas) . . . Imagine if I'd been hung over then?

He looks up at the clock. "Where's Carole?"

Nicky's beloved girls from left to right: Anita, Carole, Simone and Lynsay (Baby Lynsay, not Naughty Lindsay!).

"Don't worry, she'll be here," I say, but I don't feel so confident. I last saw her in Johnny's Bar at four this morning; we had been dancing with a couple of English house painters who'd been eyeing us from the bar at the start of the night.

"Please," Carole had said. "Is this what single life has come to?"

After the fourth vodka and tonic our compatriots were transformed into two attractive, amusing men. By three A.M. we were being spun around the empty bar-room floor. I was dancing with the uglier one when he whispered, "I really love my wife, but I feel like you could be my soulmate." I was flattered and snogged him passionately.

My first job in the morning is to take the chairs off the tables. They are stacked there every night so the floor can be mopped. Then the tablecloths need to be wiped. Big Jimmy is signing for a delivery, so I ask Eddie, "*Trapos,* please," this means "rags" in Spanish, or at least I think it does. Eddie is Ecuadorian. He is handsome, clean-looking, and very soft.

"How are you?" he asks, putting a pile of steaming *trapos* on the counter. "You sick?"

"*Poquito,*" I say. I think this is Spanish too.

I clean the Laura Ashley floral tablecloths. I pick up peas and wipe off a big smear of steak and mushroom pie from the night before when Lindsay was working. No doubt she spent most of the night sitting on the customers' laps. I have to ask Big Jimmy for the tub of sugar so I can fill up the sugar bowls.

"What you do last night?" he asks, sniffing a hangover and a story behind it.

"Nothing really. Watched some telly and went to bed."

Big Jimmy doesn't like to know that something might have gone on without him. He'd never in a million years want to come out with us, but it bothers him that we might be having a good time. (By the way, Big Jimmy is so called for no other reason than we have another chef called Jimmy who is small, and therefore named Little Jimmy.) When Big Jimmy started as a dishwasher, he couldn't speak a word of English. In between scrubbing pans and peeling potatoes, he often helped Nicky, who was the sole cook at the time. One day Jimmy went ahead and made shepherd's pie. Nicky was so impressed that she decided to train him to be a chef. For months all you could hear were Nicky's screams, "Listen to me you Brazilian bastard!" Finally, Big Jimmy mastered the art of British cuisine, curbing his native temptation to spice up every dish with peppers and garlic. When Nicky was satisfied, she came out of the kitchen and Big Jimmy got his official chef whites. The problem was she'd reared a monster in the process. I once reminded him of how sweet he used to be, how once we'd taken the subway together and he'd bought me a token.

"Did I?" He tried to remember. "You owe me a dollar then!"

I fill up ten sugar bowls and put them on the table. The salt and pepper shakers need refilling, but that entails removing the tiny corks and fiddling around with a plastic funnel. I'm in no condition to carry out such a complicated task. Let Lindsay do them.

At nine-twenty, Carole arrives. She looks around for Nicky, the boss. When she sees she's not here she relaxes. "I look terrible. Don't I?"

"Look at me!" I say.

"All right, all right. It's not all about you."

Carole never gets hangovers. She's only five foot two but she can put away more alcohol than anyone I know. The next day she wakes up ravenous. Within an hour, she'll be scoffing down a full English break-fast: eggs, bacon, sausage, mush-rooms, tomatoes and toast. Carole came to T&S just a few months after me, from the south of England like me. Back home, she was a hairdresser giving perms and blue rinses to little old ladies. Then one day she wrote a screenplay and, with her friend Zandra, came to New York to make her fortune. Like me, they're still waiting. Any-

way Carole has a theory that hangovers are due solely to guilt. I think there's some truth to that, but this morning I'm feeling a lot more than just guilt.

"What happened?" I ask.

"What do you mean what happened? I left right after you. I ought to ask you what happened." She then breaks into laughter. "You snogged him."

"Carole. If you dare say anything . . ."

"I'm not going to say anything. Please! I'd rather forget."

"I've got a really bad hangover. I want to do the back."

"Good idea. The way you look, we'll only lose tips if you're out front."

"Doing the back" means staying behind the counter to make the drinks and cream teas. If it gets very busy you might have to venture out, bus a table, take an order or the money for a check. I find the back relaxing. I love scooping the loose tea out of the caddies: the exotic whiff of jasmine, black currant, strawberry-kiwi; the earthy, Oriental fragrance of Earl Grey and Lapsang Souchong. I hold the teapot under the hot-water nozzle and stand there daydreaming in a mist of steam, a free facial while I fantasise about my brilliant future. It's the same basic fantasy: young Englishwoman, me, becomes famous actress in New York. I try not to dwell too much on the details. That would mean thinking about stuff like acting classes, auditions, head shots. These are things I intend to get organized about, but . . . I'm still not ready. I've only been in New York six months.

Jean and Shelley, both regulars since we opened and still in love after forty-six years of marriage.

There are five minutes left before Tea & Sympathy opens and the locals of Greenwich Village arrive at their favourite English café. We work without talking: laying the cutlery, emptying the big brown bag of seven-grain and white rolls, making fresh coffee, taking the cooled scones off the baking trays and putting them into brown paper bags, and arranging the freshly baked cakes under the stands. The bank is counted. The

numbers of the checks noted. We are ready for
another Sunday at the coalface.

At nine-thirty, in walks Robert carrying
The New York Times. He looks around, pleased
that he's the first customer. He sits on table
six. He moves the salt, pepper and sugar to
one side and then spreads his newspaper on
the table. When Big Jimmy sees Robert he
begins making his breakfast. On weekends
Robert has scrambled eggs with bacon and
grilled tomatoes. After this he has an order of
seven-grain toast with one pat of butter and
apricot jam. The toast mustn't be well done.

I make Robert a pot of Typhoo. My hands
know automatically where the different teas

The quintessential Robert pose—
our most regular customer and one of the family.

are. An order of Lapsang produces a minor glitch for Carole and me as neither of us are tall
enough to reach to the back of the shelf. Mostly the orders are for Typhoo and Earl Grey.
If I get an order for three cream teas with, say, rosehip, peppermint and apple-mango, I
know it will be a table of Asians. I usually pretend we're out of vanilla tea because the smell
makes me sick, hangover or no hangover.

For Robert's tea I pick a big Brown Betty, simple and classic. There are at least seven-
teen teapots from which to choose. Nicky has an army of old women scouring the flea mar-
kets and tag sales of Massachusetts for teapots and chinaware. Every three months she makes
a trip to Mass. to pick everything up. We all have our favourite teapots. Some customers go
crazy for the cow teapot while others like the little painted cottages. Up to a week ago we
used the teapots and cups from Nicky's personal collection. Many are irreplaceable and, un-
fortunately, at least one would break or disappear weekly. Her decision to remove her pre-
cious teapots came after an incident involving my favourite teapot, a rose-pink beauty with
tiny gold flowers. I always made my tea in this pot and drank from the matching cup and
saucer. Anyway, Big Jimmy, who has eyes like a hawk, saw a woman put the teapot in her
handbag (after she'd drunk the tea). Nicky confronted her, and told her to please put it back

on the table. The woman did so. Nicky was so embarrassed by the confrontation that she couldn't face the woman again. Five minutes later when the customer left we found she'd taken the teapot with her. (These were the days before we befriended the cops of the Sixth Precinct.)

Robert's Typhoo is ready and I take it to his table. Once I used the monkey teapot. "Please," he said, "don't ever serve me tea in that hideous pot."

But I love the monkey pot. A little monkey clings to green and white porcelain leaves, his paws meeting underneath the spout. There's something sad about the monkey—he has a gaunt, dignified face, and his eyes gaze into the distance. It's as if he has climbed the mast of a ship and is searching a vast ocean for a sighting of home.

Robert touches the place on his newspaper where he wants me to put his teapot, milk and cup and saucer. He looks up at me.

"Heavens! Look what the cat's dragged in," he says. "You haven't even brushed your hair."

"Yes, I did, actually."

"Well, then, I apologize."

I smile to show there are no hard feelings. I figure that's what happens when you're an interior designer: Everything becomes a question of aesthetics.

The next customer is English James, from the world of finance. Saturday's *Financial Times* and *Guardian* are under his arm. He nods at Robert and then sits on table four, the window table. He takes off his smoking jacket and peers at us through his thick-lensed glasses. He gives a quick smile. "Ashtray please, girls."

Carole takes him an ashtray.

"I'll have my usual please, Carole."

James is in his fifties. He is short and fat, with stained teeth and a baby-pink complexion. He orders baked beans (on white toast) and a pot of Earl Grey tea. He lights up a cigarette and hunches over the papers. As I'm making his tea I watch him. Within the minute he's picking his nose.

"He's off," I say to Carole.

She looks at him and turns away. When I first pointed out James's habit to Nicky she was suitably disgusted. For a few weeks she went around with a stern face, mostly galled by the fact he was doing it at the window table—she was afraid it would scare off potential customers passing by in Greenwich Avenue. What mollified her, I think, was the fact he has an upper-class accent.

At that moment I see Nicky walking down Jane Street.

"Music," I say.

Carole quickly flicks on the CD. Tom Jones booms through the restaurant. Robert looks up appalled. I turn it off. Nicky flips out if she walks in and there's no classical music playing. Tom Jones is for later in the day when the English arrive for their roast beef.

Nicky crosses Greenwich Avenue. Under her arm is a bundle of British tabloids—The Daily Mail, The Sun, and The Daily Express—all full of the latest gossip on John Major and Lady Di. It's a bright fall day, as they say on this side of the pond, and her long black hair catches the sun.

"Morning, Robert," Nicky says as she comes through the door. She then sees James. "Baked beans and no ketchup?"

I bend down and get a jar of Heinz. Nicky walks over and grabs it out of my hand. She's got that "I-have-to-do-everything" face. After Nicky's given James his ketchup she goes to table one and starts moving it about.

"You girls!" She shakes her head. "Who are you expecting? A party of bloody Biafrans? It's physically impossible for a customer to fit here." She drags the table away from the wall.

"I have to do this," she tells James and Robert. "If I don't, the customers will move them around, and that really pisses me off."

Carole and I watch from behind the counter.

"Anal cow," says Carole.

"What's wrong with you? You look dreadful," Nicky says as she joins us behind the counter.

"I think I've got food poisoning," I hold my stomach. Carole sniggers.

"Jimmy! Advil." Nicky raps on the hatch.

"Good morning to you too," says Big Jimmy, throwing her a box of Advil. Nicky passes me the box and I take two.

Outside, a flushed Mary waddles past the window.

"She gets on my nerves," Carole says as Mary walks through the door. This is Carole's way of saying she wants me to serve her. I go to the coffee machine and pour a black coffee. I get three packets of Equal and a menu. Mary plonks herself on table five, the other window table. She sits next to Robert, who ignores her. Mary is in her fifties and overweight, but her face is still beautiful: It's an Irish face, with creamy skin and eyes the colour of bluebells.

"You read me like a book, kid," she says when I bring her coffee. "I don't know whether to have the sausage sandwich?"

"Why not, if you feel like it?"

"It's not what the doctor ordered. It's got too much cholesterol."

I look over the menu for an alternative. "How about the porridge then?"

Her face falls. "You have to treat yourself sometimes. Right?"

"I can't see that one little sausage can hurt," I say. "Have it on the seven-grain bread."

"No, I'll have it on the white. Who cares? It's not as if I have a man waiting for me."

"Well," I say, "you never know."

Mary shakes her head. "I'll let you in on a little secret, kid." She beckons for me to come closer. I put my hand on the table and bend down.

"I've never had a man," she confesses in a loud whisper.

"What do you mean?"

"I'm still a virgin."

Robert draws up his newspaper.

"But you can't be?" I say looking into her blue eyes.

"I can and I am. I've never been 'you know' by a man." She giggles. "There's no need to look so shocked."

"I am. A virgin? That's terrible!"

"Well if you've never had it you can't miss it. You see, I was terrified. My mother was very strict, you know, Irish Catholic. She put the fear of God into me. Every time I got close to a man—and I've had my moments—I'd be scared to death. Whenever a man came near me with his . . ."

"Did you forget my water?" Robert says. His newspaper crashes down hitting his teapot. His green eyes are glinting.

"You go and get his water," Mary says. "And order me that sausage sandwich, kid."

I drop Mary's check on the hatch. Then I crouch down behind the counter by the breadbaskets.

"Carole," I whisper. "Come here, quick."

Carole's in the middle of giving James his free refill of Earl Grey. She turns off the water nozzle and joins me.

"What?"

"You'll never guess what Mary just told me."

Carole's brown eyes widen. "What?"

"She's a virgin!"

"No!"

"I swear. She said she's never 'had' a man."

We look at each other and then burst into uncontrollable laughter. I have to hold onto the shelf so as not to fall over. After a few minutes, Carole tries to get up to finish James's tea but collapses onto the floor.

"What on earth is up with you two?" Nicky stands above us shaking her head.

I take a napkin and wipe my eyes. Carole pulls Nicky down.

"Mary is a virgin," she says crying. "She just told Anita."

"No!" Nicky's hand flies to her mouth. "That's terrible!" She stands up and looks over at Mary. "How tragic."

Nicky's reaction sobers us. We both stand up. Mary is gazing out of the window. Robert's newspaper surrounds him like a shield.

"There must be someone we can fix her up with," says Nicky.

"Mr. Tooting!" I say.

Henry Tooting has just sat down at table two. He's English and with his handlebar moustache looks like a retired army officer. He wears blue pants with

The site of Tea & Sympathy circa 1960.

The Lady Bunny is our next-door neighbor and a favorite in the shop.

matching tunic, a bit like a French workman. When the weather gets warmer he wears a beige safari outfit. His diet also changes according to the seasons. When I first started at T&S in the summer he ordered Scotch egg and iced tea. Now the weather is colder it's Welsh rarebit and a pot of Ceylon.

The kitchen bell rings and Big Jimmy puts the sandwich on the hatch. I pick it up.

"Hey!" Nicky stops me. "Tell her to take it easy with that sausage," she guffaws with dirty laughter.

The restaurant quickly fills up with the regular Sunday breakfast crowd. For the next hour, against the background din, I make endless pots of tea. I'm on automatic pilot as Nicky and Carole shout out the tea orders. Luckily, no one orders vanilla.

A man looking a bit worse for wear limps into the restaurant. It's a moment before I realize it's Lady Bunny, New York's most famous drag queen and founder of Wigstock. I take over a menu.

"A large coffee, honey," he whispers in his Tennessee drawl. Carole and I met him last night on the street as he was on his way to DJ at Uncle Charlie's, a gay club on Greenwich Avenue. He was tottering past Johnny's Bar on six-inch heels and bursting the seams of a glamorous red dress. This morning, however, minus curly wig, false eyelashes, makeup and massive bosom, Lady Bunny looks like a chubby, blue-eyed, blond angel.

"Why are you limping?"

"It's my lower back," he says. "It comes and goes."

"I have the same problem. I find swimming really helps."

"Swimming? Won't the chlorine change my hair to some ghastly shade?"

"No," I laugh. "You just wear a swimming cap."

"Gracious! Wear a swimming cap? I'd rather walk with a limp."

♦ ♦ ♦

The kitchen bell keeps ringing. I look over and see a plate of bangers and mash on the hatch. Carole and Nicky are taking orders.

"What table?" I ask Jimmy.

"Table eleven," he says.

There isn't a table eleven, so I ignore him and look through the checks. It's for table three. My stomach lurches at the smell and sight of the dollop of mash and two fat sausages swimming side by side in rich onion gravy. I don't even look at the customer's face. Instead I rush to the bathroom. The bathroom is so tiny that if you needed to you could sit on the toilet and be sick in the wash basin at the same time. On the wall is a cardboard cutout of Prince Charles in a kilt. The sporran has been lifted by so many curious toilet-goers that it's hanging off. There is a dartboard facing me and up on the ceiling is an extractor fan. Lindsay often sits in here and has a cigarette. I rest my head in my hands and close my eyes.

After five minutes there is a rapping on the door and Nicky's asking if I'm all right. I splash my face but I can't tell if I look any better because the bathroom walls are painted black and it is dark.

The restaurant has gone into a quiet phase. Two tables are empty. There is a big Brown Betty and three mugs on table one. It must be Typhoo because that's the only tea Nicky drinks. She pours me a cup and tells me to sit down. She's already put the milk in the mugs so the tea is the same colour as a digestive biscuit. I take a sip and feel it course through me. Instant hangover relief.

Carole's joking with two gay men as she takes their order. She has a curvy little body, her breasts pert under a little black T-shirt. I think of all the cigarettes I smoked and all the money I spent just to feel rotten this morning. I could have gone to the theatre. I could have stayed in and read. Even prepared a monologue so I can start auditioning. I have to stop seeing Carole socially. It's time to change, time to take my dreams seriously. I haven't come all the way to America to end up in an English teashop serving spotted dick (with extra custard), have I?

Mr. Tooting is sitting on the next table. He leans forward. "You're wasting your time in here young lady," he says.

I experience a weird thrill. My God! Is my talent so obvious?

Sunday Morning in the Village ♦ 23

A sketch of Tea & Sympathy by Don Perlis.

He continues in a low voice. "What you should do is get yourself a job in a Catholic girls' school. Teaching is a respectable vocation and you get bags of holiday. I did it myself when I was a young chap."

"But I want to be an actress!"

"Impossible profession. You have to be star quality to get anywhere. Of course when I worked at Pinewood Studios . . ."

Nicky puts down a plate with two slices of white buttered toast. "Try eating something. It will make you feel better."

Carole passes and gives my arm a rub, "Feeling better?"

No thanks to you, I feel like saying. I start eating my toast. Nicky stands behind me eating a plate of eggs and bacon off the small podium where the menus and bank are kept. The bank is a new acquisition. It's a metal box. Up to a few weeks ago Nicky was keeping the night's take in a teapot. We always left it on the top shelf, and in the morning Nicky emptied it. There was never any question of putting the money in a bank because we'd only make enough for Nicky to buy the necessary daily groceries. One morning Robert was having difficulty pouring himself a cuppa. Thinking the leaves had clogged the spout, he opened the lid to give it a stir and found a twenty-dollar bill swimming around. We must have been busier than usual and accidentally used the bank-pot. He was most put out when Nicky asked for the twenty dollars back.

James waddles across the restaurant and stands by our table. He's left his newspapers in a heap on his chair. Under his arm is a book. I crane my neck to read the title: *Kierkegaard in Five Minutes*. It's a shame, I think, that he doesn't apply the same time-saving methodology to his nose.

"You off?" Nicky says with a mouthful of food. "Carole! Check for James."

"Look, I'll have to pay next time, Nicky," James pats his pockets. "I seem to have come out without any cash."

"No problem," she says.

I look over and catch Carole's eye. Two times out of three, James hasn't any money to pay his check. It means he gets out of paying a tip because he comes and pays the following week, conveniently forgetting the tip. Not that it's worth losing sleep over; he only ever leaves a dollar.

It suddenly dawns on me that I'm not likely to be discovered in Tea & Sympathy. People come here for their own personal reasons. Why only last week one of the regulars told me that when he confided to his therapist that he'd found refuge in a little English teashop in the Village, his therapist replied, "Oh yes. Quite a few of my patients go there."

Bubble & Squeak

Originally this dish was made with meat, but over time it has become the name for any kind of vegetable leftovers fried together. I like to use a combination of Brussels sprouts and cabbage, but you can use leeks and carrots or turnips. The name came from the noise it makes as it is frying.

SERVES 4

PREPARATION TIME: 1 hour and 15 minutes

4 tablespoons oil
1 onion, peeled and chopped
1 lb. potatoes, peeled, cooked, mashed, and seasoned
3 cups cooked cabbage and Brussels sprouts,
    finely chopped
Salt and pepper

- In a frying pan, heat 2 tablespoons oil. Add the onions and sauté them over medium heat until they are soft but not brown.
- In a bowl, mix the potatoes, cabbage, sprouts and onions; season to taste.
- Heat the remaining 2 tablespoons of oil in the same pan over medium heat.
- Add the vegetables to the pan and press the mixture evenly into a pattie. Cook over medium heat until the bottom is brown, 10–15 minutes.
- Holding a large plate over the pan, flip the plate and pan over, turning the pattie out onto the plate.
- Add the remaining oil to the pan. When it is hot, return the pattie, browned side up, to the pan and cook until the bottom is brown, about 10 minutes.
- Cut pattie into wedges and serve with fried eggs, sausage, or roasted meat, if you like.

Welsh Rarebit

Rarebit, a fancy version of cheese on toast, originated in Wales as far back as the fourteenth century. The Welsh call it *Welsh rabbit*. Over the centuries many versions have been created, some using vinegar or beer and some with additions like buck rarebit, which is Welsh rarebit topped with a poached egg. This is a versatile recipe; you may add several teaspoons of Worcestershire sauce, anchovies, scallions or any kind of onion to the mix.

SERVES 4

PREPARATION TIME: 30 minutes

5 cups grated sharp Cheddar cheese*
2 egg yolks
1 tablespoon mustard (Dijon or stronger)
1/4 cup heavy cream
Salt and pepper
6 bread slices
tomato slices (optional)
Small bunch watercress, washed and trimmed (optional)

*Vermont Cheddar is ideal and easy to find.

♦ Mix the cheese, egg yolks, mustard, cream and salt and pepper to taste into a spreadable paste.
♦ Toast one side of each bread slice, then spread the other side evenly with the mixture. I like mine spread thinly, but you may use as much as you like. Just remember that it is quite rich.
♦ Place bread slices under a hot grill (or preheated broiler) for a few minutes, until bubbling and brown.
♦ Serve topped with tomato slices and garnish with watercress, if desired.

Kedgeree

*T*his breakfast dish of fish and rice originated in India and was a favourite among British colonials. My mum made this all the time, so it is one of my favourites from my childhood. If you do not like curry flavor, you can make it without, or if you are a curry fanatic, you can spice it up.

SERVES 6–8

PREPARATION TIME: 1 hour

2 lbs. smoked haddock or finnan haddie
    (as it is sometimes called)
A few black peppercorns
1 sprig parsley
1 bay leaf
1 slice lemon
1/4 cup (1/2 stick) butter
1 cup chopped onion
1 lb. long-grain rice
2 tablespoons curry powder
Salt & pepper
4 hard-boiled eggs, peeled and quartered
Chopped parsley for garnish

- Put the fish, peppercorns, parsley sprig, bay leaf and lemon into a pan; add enough water to cover. Bring to a boil and simmer gently until the fish is tender, about 10 minutes.
- Carefully transfer the cooked fish to a large plate; let cool. Strain the mixture left in the pan. Discard the solids and reserve the stock. (If you do not have 5 cups of fish stock, add water.)

- Debone the cooled fish and flake it.
- Melt the butter in a deep pan and sauté the onion until soft. Add the rice and fish stock; bring to a boil. Reduce the heat to low and simmer about 20 minutes, until the rice is cooked.
- When the rice is cooked, add the fish, curry powder, salt and pepper to taste and 3 of the eggs; toss to combine.
- Transfer the mixture to a warm serving dish and garnish with the remaining egg and chopped parsley.

Baked Rice Pudding

At school, we would have homemade baked rice pudding. At home, we would usually have canned. I love both. You can add raisins during the last 20 minutes of cooking time or serve it with a spoonful of jam or golden syrup in the center of the pudding.

SERVES 6

PREPARATION TIME: about 3 hours

1/2 cup pudding (short-grain) rice
1/4 cup sugar
2 tablespoons butter
5 cups whole milk
Freshly ground nutmeg or cinnamon

- Preheat the oven to 300°F.
- Butter a shallow 8 x 8 or 6 x 10-inch baking dish. Add the rice, sugar and butter. Stir in the milk and sprinkle with a little nutmeg (about 1/2 teaspoon).

- Bake for about 3 hours, stirring once after 30 minutes, then once or twice over the next 2 hours, until the rice is tender and the pudding has a thick creamy consistency. If you want the skin over the top, do not stir during the last 30 minutes of baking.
- Serve either hot or cold.

CHAPTER TWO

Meeting Nicky

My first time in Tea & Sympathy, I was sitting drinking a cup of tea when a podgy little man with a mop of white curls and thick-rimmed glasses came through the door. He pulled after him a low cart full of newspapers.

"Hello, Billy. Come for your shepherd's pie?" Nicky greeted him.

"Look, Nicky! I've got bigger." He patted his belly, which flopped out of a stained T-shirt and hung over his jeans. His voice was high-pitched and nasal. There were only three other customers in the restaurant. Two old women, who I think were a little hard of hearing, were carefully spreading clotted cream on their scones. The other customer, who was sitting on the table next to me, was what Americans call preppy: He had short blond hair and was neatly dressed. At the sight of Billy, his face got pinched and red. This was Robert.

Nicky went into the kitchen to make the shepherd's pie. Billy sat down at a table, his back to the door. From under the newspapers he pulled out a small transistor radio, which he then placed between the male and female cow, salt and pepper shakers. He tucked a

Nicky with Jemima, who went back to England, became a published novelist, and used us as the backdrop for her first book (with all the names changed, of course).

paper napkin into the neckline of his T-shirt and sat with a knife in one hand and a fork in the other, his hands curled into fists. While the shepherd's pie was in the oven, Nicky came out and put in front of him a basket of white rolls with plenty of butter pats and a glass of ginger beer.

"I'm putting on weight, aren't I Nicky?" Billy asked, cramming his mouth with the soft doughy bread.

"Of course you are." Nicky spoke to him like he was a child who needed reassuring. I noticed he wore a blue plastic wristband like the kind hospitals issue.

Out of the kitchen Nicky brought a pie dish topped full of golden mash potatoes and a large pile of fresh green garden peas. It smelled delicious, and I watched hungrily as Billy tucked in. His face was only centimeters above the plate and his glasses fogged up from the steam.

"He came in one day," Nicky told me, ". . . and he said, 'Please can you help me get fat. Only I don't have any money.' 'No problem,' I said. 'I'll fatten you up.' He's been coming ever since. I can't say I see much change though. He's always been that size. I try and humour him. He's a sweet man but he's a bit . . ." She tapped the side of her head. "You know."

At this point an extremely tall man stuck his nose in the door. He looked around the teashop and asked if there was a garden. Nicky guffawed loudly.

"A garden? You'll be bloody lucky."

"You mean this is it?" The man looked incredulous.

"What you see is what you get, mate." Nicky replied.

The man said thanks and closed the door. He took one last look through the window before going off.

"He wouldn't have been able to get his legs under the table." Nicky said.

She was right. To a man that size Tea & Sympathy must be like a doll's house.

Nicky cleared away Billy's plate wiping up the peas that lay sprawled over the table-cloth. He'd screwed his napkin in a ball and put it into his empty pie dish.

"Treacle pudding with lashings of hot custard?" she asked him.

It sounded to me like something out of an Enid Blyton book, *The Famous Five Go Mad in New York*.

"Thank yooo!" Billy squealed in delight.

Nicky went off to the kitchen with a big smile on her face.

Robert leaned over and said in a low voice. "I don't know why she lets him in. He's a thoroughly odious little man."

"Nicky said he's a bit . . ." I tapped the side of my head.

"Oh phooey," said Robert. He rolled his eyes in exasperation and looked back down at his newspaper.

After Billy had finished his treacle pudding, he took a tape measure from his cart and began winding it around his belly.

"What does it say? What does it say?" He jumped up and down excitedly. Nicky went over and peered down at his belly.

"Well done," she said. "Sixty-four inches."

"Look! This is what I want to be." He held out the two ends of the tape measure as far as his podgy arms would stretch.

"Don't worry," Nicky reassured him. "You'll get there. But, like everything, it takes time."

Billy left, dragging his cart out the door into the sunshine. Nicky and I watched him waddle off down Greenwich Avenue.

"The thing is," Nicky said dramatically, "Billy is like Rain Man: He's an idiot savant!"

The only reason I was sitting there watching this scene unfold was because of a chance encounter with Nicky on my first day at the New York Health & Racquet Club. Flush with

Sean and Rosie. Rosie truly believes that she is Sean's wife rather than Nicky.

an unexpectedly large gift of money from an aunt who lived in Vienna, I decided to join one of the swankiest gyms in town, only to spend the morning wandering around it, lost. One of the recruiting staff had offered to give me an orientation tour but out of embarrassment I'd said no. Now I was too scared to ask anyone for help in case they said, "Well didn't you have an orientation?" It was full of professionals serious about working out (the kind of place where people tap you on the shoulder if you're hogging the treadmill). Finally I poked my head into a room where people in trendy workout gear stood in front of these little raised platforms. A woman was stretching by the door.

"Excuse me. What class is this?"

"Step," the woman said, and stopped stretching.

"Oh." I didn't have a clue what "step" was.

"Try it. It's great for your arse."

"Oh, you're English too," I said, surprised. With all her black curly hair piled on top of her head, and full lips covered in bright red lipstick, I thought she was Spanish. She had a good body, a nice curvy bust and longish legs. In her black leotard and leggings, she looked like a dancer.

"Where are you from?" she asked, with a noticeable London accent.

The first three girls: Alison in the middle, Carole to her right and Anita to her left. A regular customer made the uniforms, but the girls wouldn't have them for long!

"Crawley," I said, referring to the uninspiring new town south of London where I'd grown up.

"Crawley?" she said, screwing up her face. "You poor cow!"

She then gave this real bellyache of a laugh and walked off to the back of the room to get me a step.

"My name's Nicky," she said, putting my step in front of hers. "I've just opened an English restaurant in the West Village. You ought to pop in. You can get all your favourite nosh: baked beans on toast, Welsh rarebit, bangers and mash. You'll love it."

"It sounds great, " I said. I had the feeling

that she was probably bullshitting. Despite her outgoing, confident manner, she looked too young to have a restaurant. She was only a couple of years older than me and it seemed inconceivable that anyone my age could get it together to have a restaurant. It was more likely that she wanted to own a restaurant. New Yorkers always introduce themselves as artists, actors, and writers, but when it comes down to it, they are waiters, waiters, and waiters. In fact if she asked me what I did, I intended to say actress, as opposed to recently fired hostess. Until a few days ago I'd been working at the Royalton Hotel, on West 44th Street, another swanky establishment full of designer furniture and beautiful people. I'd actually been fired once before but when I went to collect my money, the manager who had fired me had also been fired. The new manager just looked at his watch and said, "You're late." So I went back to work. This time I was fired for wearing a tablecloth and pretending to be a ghost—a silly prank aimed at getting a few laughs from a Bangladeshi busboy named Ahmed, who in turn risked his job by making me forbidden cappuccinos piled high with froth.

Big Jimmy with Abe the vegetable man, who found the restaurant space for Nicky.

At the end of the step class I was knackered. I'd spent most of the hour flailing around, completely unable to keep up. I could barely even see. Nicky took my step and put it back with the others.

"Don't forget to pop your head in."

"Maybe I could get a job there?" I said, largely for something to say. She had brown eyes and an intense expression. "Yes, maybe," she replied, looking me over. "Anyway, come and have a cup of tea on the house."

After the step class I'd gone home and found a message on my machine. A very cold male voice told me that Chemical Bank wanted to see me urgently. It turned out that when I'd exchanged my aunt's Austrian schillings, the teller had accidentally given me the exchange rate for Australian dollars. Three thousand dollars suddenly became three hundred again and the bank wanted the extra returned immediately. That was of course quite impossible. I'd spent it.

So I sat in Tea & Sympathy, feeling like Alice in Wonderland and tucking into exactly the same meal Billy had enjoyed (mine was also on the house). Never in my life had I tasted such a delicious shepherd's pie. To be honest I'd never given English food a second thought. My mother was French and had never cooked traditional English meals, so my only experience had been through stodgy school dinners. I was brought up believing that English food was terrible. Tasting Nicky's shepherd's pie made me see that my mum, like me, had never had the pleasure of tasting proper British home cooking. *If I ever work here,* I thought, pouring myself another cup of tea, *I'll stay until I've tried every dish on the menu.*

"Do you still want a job?" Nicky asked.

"Yes, please," I said.

"Monday morning, eleven o'clock. Don't be late."

Postscript: I started work the following week and soon worked my way through the entire selection. Podgy Billy came in regularly for several more years until one day, when Nicky was away in England, Big Jimmy decided to serve him a Diet Coke and green salad. He let out a holler and ran out of the restaurant, never to be seen again. Nicky didn't find this out until years later and often remarked, "I wonder what happened to that idiot savant?"

Shepherd's Pie

*T*his is probably the most famous dish from England. The name refers to the shepherd and his flock of sheep. Traditionally the dish is made with lamb. At the restaurant, we serve both lamb and beef versions, but we prefer beef.

SERVES 4–6

PREPARATION TIME: 2 1/2 hours

1 medium onion, peeled and finely chopped
1 tablespoon vegetable oil
1 teaspoon butter
1 lb. lean ground beef
2 cups crushed tomatoes
1 1/4 cups beef stock
3 tablespoons Worcestershire sauce
2 teaspoons oregano
3 bay leaves
Salt and pepper
4 medium carrots, peeled, chopped, and cooked
1 1/2 cups frozen peas, cooked
Mashed potato (see page 93)
Grated sharp Cheddar cheese (optional)
Small bunch watercress, washed and trimmed (optional)

♦ Preheat the oven to 350°F.
♦ Sauté the onion in the oil and butter until it is soft.
♦ Increase heat to high, add the ground beef, and cook until completely browned, separating the meat as it is cooking to avoid winding up with big chunks of meat in the pie.

- Add tomatoes, stock, Worcestershire, oregano and bay leaves, and simmer, stirring occasionally, for about 1 hour, until the meat is tender.
- Add salt and pepper to taste, and add a little more Worcestershire sauce, if needed.
- Transfer the mixture to an ovenproof baking dish and mix in the cooked carrots and peas.
- Top with an even layer of mashed potatoes and a little grated cheese (optional). Bake for 30–40 minutes, until the top is golden brown.
- Serve garnished with watercress, if you like.

Lentil Casserole

This is a very hearty vegetarian dish, although you may add sliced cooked sausages at the end of cooking. This also makes a fantastic vegetarian shepherd's pie: Just top with mashed potatoes and brown it under a grill or broiler for a few minutes.

SERVES 6

PREPARATION TIME: 1 1/2 hours

1 eggplant, peeled and cut into 1/2-inch cubes

2 tablespoons olive oil

1 onion, peeled and chopped

2 cloves garlic, peeled and chopped (optional)

4 carrots, peeled and chopped

2 stalks celery, chopped

2 medium parsnips, peeled and cut into 1-inch strips

1 cup and 2 tablespoons whole green or brown lentils

3 3/4 cups hot vegetable stock or water

2 bay leaves

1 sprig parsley
1 teaspoon dried savoury or oregano
1 teaspoon herbes de Provence
2 tablespoons tomato puree
Salt and freshly ground black pepper

- Preheat the oven to 375°F.
- Sauté the eggplant in 1 tablespoon of the olive oil until it is soft and set aside.
- Heat the remaining tablespoon of oil in a large flameproof casserole and sauté the onion until soft.
- Add the garlic and cook 5 minutes. Stir in the carrots, celery, parsnips and lentils, then pour in the hot stock or water. Bring to a boil and simmer for 10 minutes.
- Add the bay leaves, parsley, oregano, *herbes de Provence* and the cooked eggplant, then add the tomato puree and salt and pepper to taste.
- Cover tightly with foil and bake, stirring occasionally, for 35–45 minutes.
- Check to see if all of the vegetables are tender and if the water has been completely absorbed. If the vegetables aren't cooked and all the water has been absorbed, add a little more hot stock or water, cover with aluminum foil again, and cook for another 15 minutes, or until the vegetables are tender and the liquid has been absorbed. Should there be too much liquid, cook, uncovered, for a few minutes.

In England we love to smother all sorts of puddings with custard. The most commonly used instant custard is made by Birds. An absolute British staple, this product can be found more and more in America. When we make it in the restaurant, we make it thick and then refrigerate it. When you need to use it, whisk it and add a little heavy cream. If you wish you can also add a few drops of vanilla extract during the preparation.

Carrot Cake

*T*his carrot cake is much darker and more moist than most, so it also makes great fairy cakes or cupcakes, but remember if you are making them individually they will take less oven time and must go in paper cases filled almost to the top before baking.

SERVES 10–12

PREPARATION TIME: 1 hour and 15 minutes

2 cups sugar
1 1/2 cups good-quality vegetable oil
4 eggs, lightly beaten
4 cups sifted all-purpose flour
1 teaspoon salt
2 teaspoons baking powder
1 1/2 teaspoons cinnamon
1 teaspoon nutmeg
1 teaspoon allspice or mixed spice

8 peeled and grated carrots (about 3 cups)
1 cup chopped walnuts
Carrot Cake Icing (see below)

- Preheat the oven to 350°F.
- Beat the sugar, oil and eggs
- Sift together the flour, salt, powder and spices.
- With a spatula, fold the flour into the egg mixture in batches, blending well after each addition. Fold in the carrots and nuts.
- Pour the batter into a greased and floured 9 1/2-inch round, 2-inch deep baking tin. Bake for about 1 hour and 5 minutes.
- Remove the cake from the oven and turn it out onto a wire rack to cool. Coat lavishly with Carrot Cake Icing (below).

CARROT CAKE ICING
8 ozs. cream cheese, softened
1/2 cup (1 stick) butter, softened
3 cups sifted confectioners' sugar
2 teaspoons pure vanilla extract

- Mash the cream cheese and the butter, adding the confectioners' sugar and vanilla a little at a time. Beat vigorously until smooth and spreadable. You can use a standing mixer, if you like.

Treacle Pudding

*T*reacle (pronounced TREE-cull) can be made with black treacle instead of golden, if you wish. There are many different variations of this pudding, some made with suet and some not. If you wish to make the really stodgy suet variety, see page 109. We use Tate & Lyle golden syrup, which is a refined sugar product that tastes similar to a cross between honey and molasses.

SERVES **8–10**

PREPARATION TIME: 45 minutes

1 recipe sponge batter for Victoria Sandwich
    (see page 57)
1 1/4 cups Tate & Lyle golden syrup
    (A little extra will do no harm.)
Hot custard, optional (page 94)

♦ Preheat the oven to 350°F.
♦ Butter and flour a 10-inch round Bundt pan.
♦ Prepare the sponge batter as instructed.
♦ Pour the syrup into the pan, then spoon in the batter, gently smoothing the top with a spatula.
♦ Bake for about 30 minutes; the sponge should be golden on top
♦ Remove the cake from the oven and let it cool for 2–3 minutes. Place a plate on top of the Bundt pan, then quickly but firmly turn the plate and pan upside down to release the cake onto the plate. You may need to loosen the edges very slightly with a knife before you flip it.
♦ Serve with hot custard, if you like.

OTHER IDEAS

For jam syrup pudding, you may substitute raspberry jam for the golden syrup.

CHAPTER THREE

A Spiritual Lift

W here on earth could she be?" said Nicky. "You checked the bathroom?"
"Yes."

Our new waitress, Tina, was missing. Three of us were working, Carole, Tina and I, and even with Nicky's help we could barely keep up. It was Saturday afternoon and the lines reached halfway down the block. Customers crowded around the windows staring in at those already eating. The pushy ones wanted to wait inside. They'd stand in their coats, blocking our way to the tables.

"You can't stand here!" Nicky snapped at them and they scuttled out. She then ranted and raved to the whole restaurant about the "unbelievable rudeness" of some customers. This had been going on for six months, ever since Bryan Miller had given us a rave review in *The New York Times*.

It was amazing, the power of a good review. Six months ago we were barely making ends meet. The oven in the kitchen, which was just a regular household oven, was tied together with a piece of string. Only two burners worked. If you were cooking soup and heating up vegetables, then you couldn't do anything else. Every morning before use it needed a good kick to make sure the wires made contact. The cooker had cost five hundred dollars, which was then a small fortune, and we'd already been through two. When we were finally down to one burner, Nicky left the door to her apartment open (she lived down the block) so the kitchen guys could traipse back and forth along Greenwich Avenue with pots of food.

The refrigerator was a donation and was also a home appliance. It was hiked up on bricks and a big lump of wood. Every time you opened the door, you needed one hand for the handle and the other for supporting the top so it wouldn't fall on your head. The other kitchen appliances were a small toaster and a microwave. We used the latter to heat desserts. Every time it was on, the lights in the restaurant dimmed like London in the Blitz.

Nothing, however, could beat the air conditioner for inefficiency. It had been in its slot above the door for about twenty years before Tea & Sympathy was ever thought of. If it weren't for an intermittent clanking you'd never know it was on. We had to keep calling

Rudi, who lived upstairs, to fix it. He was an old artist and something of a handyman. He'd come down with a cigarette hanging out of the corner of his mouth and without saying a word he'd take it out on the sidewalk. I often watched him and could never work out what he was doing. Sometimes he just stood and stared at it. After an hour he'd declare it fixed. He'd stick it back above the door and Nicky would hand him a bag of scones.

"Great!" she'd say once Rudi left. "It's one degree cooler."

In spite of all these setbacks, Nicky miraculously turned out delicious food. The problem was that customer growth was

Howard has been a customer since the beginning and not only has become one of Sean and Nicky's good friends, but is also a partner in their fish & chip shop, A Salt & Battery.

through word of mouth and not everyone wanted to tell their friends about such a tiny restaurant. They couldn't all be like Fred Schneider, the singer of the American group the B-52's, who for weeks after Nicky first opened, stood outside the empty restaurant with a cup of tea. Because he was famous, he knew people would stop and chat and take notice of us. Despite Fred's best efforts, the restaurant's future was in doubt. In an act of desperation, Nicky left an answering machine message for Bryan Miller, the then-food critic of *The New York Times*. She told him who she was and that she'd opened a British restaurant. She left the address and phone number. Six weeks later he called back and said he'd

Fred, lead singer of the B-52's, was probably the very first Tea & Sympathy customer.

been in and reviewed the restaurant and that it was going to be in *The New York Times* a week from Wednesday. "Are you ready for this?" he asked her.

Miller started off by telling his readers that the mere mention of British cuisine meant he'd approached his task with all "the enthusiasm of a traffic cop called to a five-car pile-up on the West Side Highway."

But he went on to praise every single dish he'd tried in the restaurant, and added: "For years I've been searching for an authentic shepherd's pie, and here it is, served in a big oval dish. The ground lamb was medium rare, juicy and well-seasoned, enhanced with onions and still firm carrots, all under a thick layer of mashed potatoes."

I don't think any of us were prepared for the mob scenes that began the same day. I certainly wasn't, not with my skills as a waitress. There were certain things I just couldn't do, one of which was to walk fast with a bowl of soup. Also, I couldn't hold more than one plate in each hand. I could, however, carry four teacups on one hand by sticking each finger through a handle—but removing them didn't exactly look professional.

I had discovered some shortcuts: Instead of holding the teapot under the hot water nozzle I just left it there. This gave me time to put a basket of rolls on a table, refill a sugar bowl or deliver a cream tea. Through the din of voices and clattering cutlery, it was possible to hear the jet of hot water. It changed pitch just when the teapot was almost full. Just enough time to run back and turn it off.

And now we had the added crisis of a vanished waitress!

"She could have gone to the deli," Carole said to me as she scooped ice into four ginger beers.

"I bet she's done a runner."

Her eyes widened. "No!"

It was an exciting thought, and maybe the only explanation. Today had been relentless. You couldn't pass a table without someone grabbing your arm or shoving an empty water glass in your face.

Customers were coming from all over.

Peter, a longtime regular customer and expert on military uniforms, when he came to Tea & Sympathy to celebrate the Fourth of July.

Along with our regulars were the celebrities: models, actors, sitcom stars, musicians, fashion designers. I learned to read Nicky's expression when she recognized someone. It was a way of looking without really looking. A talent perfected by her ten-year stint of waitressing in fashionable New York restaurants.

"Table four, Johnny Rotten," she'd say, without moving her lips.

Robert bought us a Polaroid camera so we could take celebrity photos and put them on the wall of fame—the short stretch of wall between the kitchen and the toilet. The day after we got the camera, Roger Daltrey of The Who came in for dinner. I decided to take a Polaroid of him. It was difficult to snap secretly because the camera was too bulky and the flash was sure to go off. But I couldn't ask him either, because I'd go really red, so I decided to write him a note. I took a blank check and on the back wrote:

Dear Mr. Daltrey,

Would it be all right if I took a photo of you? Nod if it is, or shake your head if you'd rather I didn't. Either way is fine.

Thank you for reading this,

Love . . .

Roger Daltrey in the first, and only, Tea & Sympathy Polaroid ever taken by Anita.

Writing my name seemed too intimate. He might think I fancied him. He might also feel pressured to say yes. So I crossed out the "Love" and just signed it "your waitress." I dropped it in front of his apple crumble and custard. He read the note and nodded.

As I held the picture in my hand waiting for the image to develop, I felt uneasy. In my mind's eye, I saw Roger Daltrey's expression after he'd read the note. He'd looked at me . . . well almost in fear! That was the last Polaroid I took.

◆ ◆ ◆

The only flaw in my theory that Tina had run away was that out of all of us she was the calmest. "Spacey" is probably a more apt description. She never wrote down an order, preferring to trust her memory. She'd call out the list of teas she needed and four out of five would be wrong. It meant putting four full teapots on the hatch and warning Frankie to be careful when he picked them up, and then waiting for him to clean them because I was four teapots short. To be honest, things were a whole lot smoother without her.

Earlier, when I was making drinks and she was cutting cake for an afternoon tea stand, she told me a story. She'd recently moved to an artist's loft in an old commercial building in Brooklyn. A week before, she was sitting on the toilet when a man's voice came out of nowhere.

"Who's there?" the voice asked.

"Me, Tina," she replied.

Paul Smith, center, the designer and fabulous suit maker, with Sarah from the Paul Smith New York press department and Sean, wearing a Paul Smith suit, of course.

The voice had come from a small hole in the ceiling. "Who are you?" Tina asked.

"Neil," said the voice.

By the time she'd finished her business they'd had "a profoundly spiritual conversation." These exchanges continued, taking place every day at all hours. He was a visual artist making collages. Sometimes he played her music or read prose or a poem. It was just like a relationship, Tina said, except neither of them had seen each other.

"But he's living above you. Surely you've bumped into him?"

"Never," she said. "I have no idea what he looks like."

Neil must have been wondering what she looked like, because the night before he invited her to his studio for dinner. That was to happen tonight. If she really had run off, how was I to find out what happened?

While I thought about Tina's sudden departure, Carole sat three people on table six: two Buddhist monks and a lady dressed in a business suit.

"That's all we need," says Nicky rolling her eyes. "Hare Krishnas. If they start bashing those tambourines, show 'em the door."

Robert's sitting at table seven. He keeps looking in an agitated way at the monks. Maybe he feels hemmed in. That's the trouble—table six is really a table for two except we've stuck an extra chair on the end of it.

"Everything all right, Robert?" I go and ask him.

His eyes seem to look through me. "Have you any idea who is in this restaurant?"

I'm nervous. It's like a test. I know I'm going to fail because I never recognize anyone. I shake my head no.

"Table six," he says in a low thrilled voice. "The Dalai Lama!"

"The Dalai Lama?" An animal similar to a camel flashes through my mind. I sneak a look at table six. There is something familiar about the monk with the glasses.

"Go and tell Nicky," he orders.

I hurry back. Diane, a lawyer and writer of sonnets as well as a regular customer, has hold of Nicky's arm.

"The Dalai Lama, Nicky!" Her voice was a low urgent whisper. "The frigging Dalai Lama!"

"I know, I know. Remind me again?"

"The Holy Leader of Tibet. The . . . the . . . Richard Gere's friend."

"No!" Nicky mouthed. Then a silent scream. "I don't believe it."

Within one second she picked up the phone, pounded out a few numbers, and in a low voice, breathless with emotion said, "You'll never guess who's sitting in our restaurant . . . the Dalai Lama!"

I carried the Dalai Lama's afternoon tea across the restaurant floor as if I was on a holy pilgrimage. At the table they were speaking in soft voices. I moved his cup and saucer to make room for the tea stand. I had given him my favorite teacup, the pink one with little gold flowers. The woman was drinking from the cup with a picture of a red lobster in it. On the saucer was written "Welcome to Cape Cod."

On the top tier of the three-tiered cake stand was a slice of chocolate cake, lemon cake, and a big luscious piece of Victoria sponge sandwich cake. (I had wanted to include the coffee and walnut cake, but as they were drinking chamomile tea, they probably wouldn't want the caffeine.) On the second tier were six pale scones. Underneath them were the finger sandwiches: egg salad on crusty white, smoked salmon, and cheese and pickle.

I took my time arranging the tea while my eyes feasted greedily on the

Nicky's dear friend of many years Estelle Lazarus, right, with the fabulous Cherry Vanilla.

Roger Glover of Deep Purple, with his lovely wife, Leslie, and their kids.

Dalai Lama. They followed the saffron sleeve that lay like a silk handkerchief inches from the cake stand, contrasting beautifully with the salmon peeking out of the seven-grain bread. I traveled up the bare olive of his arm to his pure broad face. His skin was unlined. His spectacles added to his air of gentle refinement. I could feel the goodness radiate from him. I wanted to speak to him, say something profound. I placed the little containers of clotted cream and strawberry preserves side by side.

"If you need more clotted cream just let me know," I said, blushing violently.

The woman looked around the table and shook her head. The Dalai Lama smiled politely. As I left I sort of walked backward. It felt odd that I couldn't bow or offer some mark of respect.

A silent undercurrent of electricity spread through the restaurant. People stared while pretending not to. Every time their eyes could wander, for example when drinking from their teacups, they drifted casually back to him. His little table carried on oblivious.

"Isn't it amazing," said Nicky. "All the vegetarian restaurants in New York and he chose to come here."

We were all standing around the podium pretending not to stare.

Diane came out of her stupor to provide us with more information. She told us how he was the thirteenth Dalai Lama, a god-king, and about the plight of the Tibetan refugees.

"We ought to send down some of our new T-shirts," Nicky said. "They've got the Tea & Sympathy logo on the front. On the back it says 'Help the Homesick.'"

I was taking another order when I saw that Carole had snuck away to clean their table. She made no attempt to actually clean the table except for removing the cake stand, which she held dangling in the air. A little bit of exposed tummy hung out of her black jeans. Even the top she wore was too small. No doubt she was blathering on about Richard Gere.

"Carole's getting on well with them," Nicky said pleased.

"That was my table."

"Buddhism's not about jealousy and possessiveness, Anita," Nicky said.

Carole came back with a daft smile. "He's such a sweetheart, bless him."

"Did you have a nice little chat?" I asked. "I'm taking the check."

"Too late," Carole smirked. "They already asked for it."

I looked over at the table and saw that the woman was examining the bill.

"You bitch!"

"Stop it you two or I'll bang your heads together. Anyway," said Nicky. "I doubt if he carries money. That thing doesn't look as if it has pockets."

"He's got amazing skin," said Carole.

"It's not cosmetic," Diane told us. "It's an inner beauty. He meditates for hours."

"I'm going to meditate," Carole said.

"Oh no!" Diane gives a loud moan. "He's leaving!"

Nicky quickly strides across the restaurant and opens the door.

"Thank you very much," she says to the lady who exits first.

"Thank you very much," she repeats to the other monk.

The Dalai Lama is last out of the door.

"It's been wonderful having you," Nicky beams at him. "Please come again."

The Dalai Lama joins his palms together and bows. After a moment's hesitation, Nicky does a strange movement, a cross between a bow and a curtsey. By the time she's lifted up her head, he's gone. Nicky closes the door. She turns around and raises her arm in a salute.

"Yes!" she shouts.

The restaurant erupts. It's as if we are all extras on a film set and the director has just called "cut" after the big action scene. A terrific din follows as everyone describes how they felt when they first realized it was the Dalai Lama. I ran over and sat on his chair. It was still warm.

"What on earth are you doing?" asked Robert.

"I'm getting a bit of the holy karma on my bum."

"Please!" said Robert. "You didn't even know who he was."

It was at that moment that Tina chose to return. She walked through the door, a serene smile on her face.

"What happened?" I asked.

"I went for a walk. You should go outside. It's a lovely autumn day, you can even hear birds singing."

Postscript: After hooking up with Neil, spacey Tina left T&S of her own free will. The last I heard she had been hired by a waiflike British supermodel as a personal assistant to help "organize her life." Meanwhile, I arrived at work a few days later limping. "I don't feel very well," I told Nicky. "The doctor says I've got hemorrhoids." She looked at me and just laughed. "Karma, my arse!" she said. "Serves you bloody well right."

Finger Sandwiches

*T*hese are a great lunch or snack and are an afternoon tea must. We serve large platters of them when we cater cocktail parties. The thinner the bread the better; however, some whole loaves are difficult to slice thinly, especially when they are very fresh, so try to choose quite dense bread when you are slicing it yourself. To help the sandwiches stay fresh before serving them, cover them with paper towel, then sprinkle the towel with a little water or wrap them in cellophane. Do not put them in the refrigerator or they will go soggy. White bread goes stale much faster than seven-grain or whole-wheat bread, so if you wish to be leisurely about eating them, use more of the dark bread than the white.

DIFFERENT FILLINGS
Chicken Salad
Tuna Salad
Egg Salad & Watercress
Cucumber & Cream Cheese

CHICKEN SALAD
1 1/2 cups cooked cold chicken (dark or white meat or mixed),
*   cut into small pieces*
1/2 cup finely chopped celery
2 teaspoons Dijon mustard
Salt and pepper
4–5 tablespoons mayonnaise

MAKES ABOUT 10 FINGERS

♦ Mix all of the ingredients together, leaving the salt and pepper until the end. You may use stronger mustard if you wish.

TUNA SALAD

2 cups canned tuna fish in oil or water, well drained
2 tablespoons onion, peeled and very finely chopped
1/2 cup finely chopped celery
1/2 cup red pepper, finely chopped
4 teaspoons balsamic vinegar
Juice of 1 lemon
5–6 tablespoons mayonnaise
Salt and pepper

MAKES ABOUT 10 FINGERS

♦ Mix all of the ingredients together, leaving the salt and pepper to the end.

EGG SALAD & WATERCRESS

6–8 hard-boiled eggs
3–4 tablespoons mayonnaise
Salt and pepper
1 bunch watercress, washed and trimmed

MAKES ABOUT 10 FINGERS

♦ Peel and chop up the eggs quite roughly.
♦ Mix with mayonnaise and add a little salt and pepper.
♦ Add a small sprig of watercress to each sandwich before cutting it.

CUCUMBER & CREAM CHEESE

Cream cheese, softened
Very thinly sliced cucumber
Salt and pepper

MAKES ABOUT 10 FINGERS

- Spread a little cream cheese on 1 side of each slice of bread, then layer cucumber to desired thickness. Season to taste.
- Top with the remaining slice.

OTHER IDEAS

You can also use thinly sliced ham and cream cheese.

TO ASSEMBLE THE FINGER SANDWICHES

- Choose a selection of good-quality thinly sliced white, whole-wheat and seven-grain breads.
- Spread 1 slice of bread with the desired filling and top with a plain slice.
- With a sharp knife cut the crusts off of the bread and discard. Cut the sandwich diagonally into triangles or finger shapes.
- Serve garnished with a sprig of fresh watercress.

Tea & Sympathy Scones

The scone was originally any type of sweet bread, rich or plain. If you read old English cookery books there are many ways to make them. At Tea & Sympathy, we stay with a very basic recipe and we do not use butter. These scones do not last until the next day, so they should be eaten within a few hours of baking, before they become dry and stale. If you are having them for tea, I suggest you make them no more than a couple of hours before you serve them, to eat them at their very best.

MAKES ABOUT 12 SCONES

PREPARATION TIME: 20 minutes

2 cups sifted all-purpose flour
1 tablespoon baking powder
2 tablespoons sugar
1 teaspoon salt
1 1/3 cups heavy cream

♦ Preheat the oven to 375°F.
♦ Sift all the dry ingredients into a large bowl.
♦ Add the heavy cream and mix gently. Do *not* overmix. If the mixture is very sloppy, add a little more flour.
♦ By hand spread out the dough on a floured surface to 1-inch thickness.
♦ Cut out scones with a two-inch cookie cutter and place them on an ungreased baking sheet. Bake for 12 minutes.
♦ Cool on a wire rack.

OTHER IDEAS

When the scones have cooked, split them in half horizontally, then smear the cut side of each half generously with clotted cream and jam.

♦ Clotted Cream ♦

You cannot buy fresh clotted cream in the United States, but you can find jars of pasteurized Devonshire cream or clotted cream that have been imported from England in gourmet stores. There is no real difference between Devonshire and clotted cream, it just means that the clotted variety comes from Cornwall and the Devonshire from Devon. If you open the jar and it has separated, just whip it up slightly to stiffen it so it doesn't drip down the sides of the scones.

Victoria Sandwich

*T*his is our most popular cake, named after Queen Victoria. It is a great afternoon tea cake because it is easy to make and nice and light to eat.

SERVES 8–10

PREPARATION TIME: 35–40 minutes

1 cup (2 sticks) unsalted butter
1 cup sugar
4 eggs
A few drops of pure vanilla extract
2 cups sifted all-purpose flour
1 heaping teaspoon baking powder

♦ Preheat the oven to 350°F.
♦ With an electric mixer, cream the butter and sugar until light and fluffy.
♦ Add the eggs, one at a time, along with the vanilla.
♦ With a spatula, fold in the flour and baking powder and mix until smooth.

- Divide the batter between 2 buttered and floured 8-inch cake tins and smooth the surface by tapping gently on the side of the tins.
- Bake 20–25 minutes.
- As with all cakes, the best way to make sure the cake is done is by inserting a thin knife or skewer into the center of the cake: If it comes out clean, then the cake is done. Turn out onto wire rack to cool.

BUTTER CREAM ICING

1/2 cup (1 stick) butter
1/4 teaspoon vanilla extract
2 cups confectioners' sugar
1–2 tablespoons milk

- In an electric mixer beat the butter until light and creamy, then add the vanilla.
- Gradually beat in the confectioners' sugar.
- Add just enough milk to make the mixture soft and spreadable.

TO ASSEMBLE THE VICTORIA SANDWICH

Raspberry Jam
Confectioners' sugar for dusting

- Once the cake has cooled, spread one half of the cake evenly with the butter cream. Spread the other half with raspberry jam.
- Put the two halves together, with the cream facing the jam, and place on a cake plate. Dust lightly with confectioners' sugar.

Sugar-Glazed Lemon Cake

My mum is a fantastic cake maker, and this is one of her favourites. It has a delicious tangy, sweet, slightly crunchy topping. I am afraid to say that we eat most of it before it gets to the customer, sorry!

SERVES 6–8

PREPARATION TIME: 1 hour and 35–50 minutes

For the cake:
3/4 cup (1 1/2 sticks) unsalted butter
3/4 cup sugar
2 large eggs, beaten
1 1/2 cups sifted all-purpose flour
1 teaspoon baking powder
Juice and zest of 2 lemons
1/4 cup whole milk

For the glaze:
1/2 cup sugar
Juice of 4 lemons

- Preheat the oven to 350°F.
- To prepare the cake: Grease and flour an 8 x 4 1/2 x 3-inch loaf tin.
- In an electric mixer, cream the butter and sugar together until light and fluffy.
- Beat in the eggs, one at a time.
- With a spatula, fold in the flour and baking powder.
- Add the lemon juice and zest and the milk a little at a time.
- Transfer the mixture to the loaf tin and bake for about 1 1/4–1 1/2 hours, until soft and spongy to the touch.

- To prepare the glaze: Gently heat the sugar and lemon juice together until the sugar has dissolved. Continue to boil for about 15 seconds.
- Pour the syrup over the cake while it is warm and let cool.

Chocolate Cake

Chocolate cake is a very passionate thing. Several times over the years, we decided to change the recipe and still people come and ask for previous versions. However, I think this is the best we have ever done. It was inspired by one of Nigella Lawson's cakes, but we do it a little differently and add the most delicious icing.

SERVES 8–10

PREPARATION TIME: 1 hour and 15 minutes

For the cake:
1 cup bittersweet plain dark chocolate
1 1/4 cups all-purpose flour
1 cup (2 sticks) butter
1 1/2 cups dark brown sugar
3 eggs, beaten
1 tablespoon vanilla extract
1 teaspoon baking soda
1 cup hot water

For the icing:
4 tablespoons milk
1/4 cup (1/2 stick) butter
1/2 cup bittersweet dark chocolate, grated

1 3/4 cups sifted confectioners' sugar
shaved chocolate (optional)

- Preheat the oven to 375°F.
- Grease an 8-inch cake tin.
- Melt the chocolate in a basin over a pan of hot water; leave to one side.
- Sift the flour and baking soda into a bowl.
- Cream the butter and sugar together until light and fluffy. Add the eggs a little at a time, and then the vanilla.
- With a spatula, fold the melted chocolate into the butter/sugar mixture, then add the flour and baking soda little by little, and then the hot water.
- Pour the mixture into a greased 8-inch cake tin and bake for 45 minutes.
- Turn the cake out onto a wire rack to cool.
- To prepare the icing: Heat the milk, butter, and chocolate gently in a saucepan until melted.
- In a medium bowl, pour the chocolate mixture onto the confectioners' sugar and beat until smooth.
- Pour on top of the cake and spread evenly with a spatula, covering the cake completely.
- Decorate the iced cake with a little shaved chocolate.

CHAPTER FOUR

The Bacon Man

W hat's wrong?" Big Jimmy asks when I arrive at work one hot August morning. "Why you early?"

"I'm early because I love my job, Jimmy."

He shakes his head and calls me a "wanker."

Big Jimmy has just come back from a holiday in England. Nicky persuaded him that as he worked in an English restaurant it would be a good idea to experience English culture. It was his first trip to Europe and it was spent entirely in an English pub. He came back with a beer belly, and now calls everyone "mate" or "wanker."

The real reason I'm early is because I was about to have a shower this morning when I saw a dead mouse poking out from underneath the curtain. I was so horrified that I threw on a dress and came straight to work.

Lindsay arrives on time at eleven.

Nicky's wonderful girls, from left to right: Jemima, Carole and Naughty Lindsay.

"It's such a beautiful day Nits. Fancy wasting it in here! We could have rented a car and gone to the beach."

"I'm on a double shift," I tell her.

She gives me a sympathetic look before going into the kitchen to kiss Big Jimmy. He likes her. Sometimes when she's working, he'll come out of the kitchen to sit on the stool by the podium and Lindsay will sit on his lap. It seems strange to see him being nice.

"I could have him," Lindsay confided to me one day.

"But he's so horrible."

"I know. That's what turns me on," she said and burst into laughter. When Lindsay laughs it's contagious. She throws her head back, claps her hand over her mouth and then snorts with her head going up and down. Her face goes red, and her blue eyes water.

A white van arrives outside Tea & Sympathy. It's the bacon man's weekly delivery of lean back Irish bacon. He is a shy Irishman with pink skin and ginger hair.

"How's your pork today?" Lindsay says with a dirty smile.

The bacon man blushes a brilliant red. He stands by the kitchen hatch waiting to be paid.

"Does your girlfriend like your pork?" Lindsay asks him as she fills up the clotted cream containers. She holds her tongue between her teeth and does this thing with her head, a sort of wobble.

He quickly says, "I don't have a girlfriend."

Lindsay bends over to put the clotted cream jars in the fridge. She angles her pert ass in his direction. He stares and then quickly looks away.

I go off to the front with a big bunch of knives and forks and start laying the tables. The restaurant opens in half an hour. I still have to fill the sugar bowls and make the iced tea, which involves filling numerous teapots. That's the one thing I hate about summer, making iced tea—I'm always trying to invent ways to make it easier.

The kitchen bell rings. Big Jimmy is glowering through the hatch, looking for the bacon man. The bacon man is now standing next to Lindsay. In order to prolong the flirting, Lindsay is making the iced tea for probably the first time in her life.

I keep away from them. Instead I walk around the restaurant straightening the pictures. It's the first time I've done this and I realize how unobservant I am. I've never really looked at what's on the walls before: an old tin advertisement for Lyons Maid ice cream, the framed original music score to the movie *Tea and Sympathy*.

And above table three is a framed poem by Ginger Baker. He came in the door one day and in a loud cockney voice recited a monologue about tea. Nicky gave him a pen and paper and he wrote down his ode to tea. When customers ask me who's Ginger Baker? I make something up like, "Oh, Ginger Baker, that's the queen's hairdresser." It was only recently that I finally asked Nicky and found out that he was the drummer for Cream and Traffic.

There is a photograph of Franklin and Eleanor Roosevelt sitting on the White House lawn with the Queen Mum and her husband, George VI. It's World War Two and they are all eating hotdogs.

There's a portrait of the queen, the young Elizabeth, a royal blue slash painted against her slender figure. I'm surprised she's still up on the wall; Nicky's not too happy with the way she's been treating poor old Di lately.

There's also a signed photograph of Chip the vicar. He came in one day in regular clothes and accidentally sat on some green bubblegum. Lindsay offered to scrape it off with a knife and when

NICKY PERRY AND THE CREW:

TEA AND SYMPATHY HATH PLEASED MY SOUL
AND COMFORTETH THE WEARY.
IN THE GREAT BRITISH TRADITION, WE ARE PROUD
TO BE LOYAL CUSTOMERS.

The Rev. Fr. A.C. Howard III
YOUR VICAR

Our favorite, Chip the vicar.

To Nicki
all good wishes
Margaret Thatcher
6 August 1997

Photo of Malcolm Forbes's yacht, inscribed to Nicki by Margaret Thatcher.

she'd finished she patted his bottom. He returned the following week wearing his dog collar.

"I can't believe I've had my hands on your bum," she said to him, mortified.

Chip told her not to worry. The bubblegum, he said, had been sent by God.

Finally, above table eight is a photograph of Forbes's private yacht, the *Highlander,* which Margaret Thatcher autographed. Toby, a regular customer, was the pilot of the helicopter that ferried VIPs to and from the yacht. Nicky is really proud because when Toby asked Maggie to sign it for her, she said knowingly, "Oh it's for the tea lady."

The bacon man finally leaves. I plan on asking Lindsay to spend the night—she can get rid of the mouse and check that there's no more around. That sort of stuff doesn't bother her; her thesis at school is something about the disposal of fecal matter in developing countries.

"Lindsay, can you stay the night? I've got a mouse problem."

"I can't, Nits," Lindsay says. "I've got a date with the bacon man."

"When?"

"Tonight. I'm meeting him here at eight. Can you believe it?" She starts to laugh.

"Do you like him?" I try and keep the amazement out of my voice.

"He's not good-looking, but he's definitely manly."

"Well you can both come and spend the night," I say.

Lindsay laughs as if I'm joking.

At five o'clock Carole arrives and Lindsay goes home to relax and change before her date. When I tell Carole about the bacon man she's not impressed.

"Imagine being touched by a man that handles raw meat?"

I know what she means.

Just before eight, Lindsay arrives in a flowery blue skirt and white cheesecloth shirt. Her blond wavy hair is loose. Carole and I look at each other surprised. Lindsay never dresses up, so we come to the conclusion that she really must like him.

"I'd love to be a fly on the wall," Carole says.

"Why don't you come back and spend the night? I've got a bottle of wine and we can keep tabs on Lindsay. It'll be a laugh."

"Brilliant," says Carole rubbing her hands together. I decide not to mention the mouse until we get home.

The regular male customers are staring at Lindsay. They've never seen her in a dress before.

"So what's the special occasion?" the psychiatrist asks her. "Who's the lucky man?"

"The bacon man," Lindsay replies. "He's not really boyfriend material, but he's very manly."

She flexes an arm to denote his masculinity.

"Give me a break," says Robert, rolling his eyes.

"Lindsay's looking very dolled up," says Mr. Tooting when I take his order. "A real dolly bird."

"She's going on a date," I explain.

"Anyone we should know?"

"The bacon man."

Mr. Tooting looks serious. "An honest living. Puts the food on the table. I used to work in the food industry. I was in charge of production at a poultry farm."

"Really, Mr. Tooting?"

"Yes. But that was long before you were born. Nice chap, is he?"

"Yes. He's very manly."

"Manly? Good, good, right you are." Mr. Tooting dives back into his newspaper.

Big Jimmy's eyes nearly pop out of his head when he sees Lindsay sitting on table one, all dressed up and smoking a cigarette.

"Where's she going?"

I am torn between telling him about the bacon man, which will knock his ego right down, or not telling him anything, and torturing him with the suspense. I decide to tell him; he'll find out anyway, and I'll get a chance to observe the misery firsthand.

"She's going on a date," says Carole, standing behind me.

"And you'll never guess who with," I say.

"Who?"

His curiosity is so naked and overwhelming. I look at Carole. We smile. As if on cue, there comes the clanking of a horn as the bacon van pulls up outside the restaurant.

"The bacon man!" we cry in unison. His jaw literally drops open.

The customers all watch as the bacon man climbs out of his van. He is wearing beige cords and a brown plaid shirt.

"Bless 'im," Carole says. The poor guy is bright red. He walks self-consciously to the door and peers in.

"He could have rented a car," says Lindsay. "The bloody bacon van, for Chrissake!"

She puts out her cigarette. "Sorry about the mice, Nits. I'll come and plug the holes up tomorrow night." She then runs out.

"What mice?" Carole turns on me suspiciously.

I pull a face as if I don't know what Lindsay's on about.

Big Jimmy is quiet for the rest of the night. At around nine o'clock, the espresso machine lets off a puff of steam and then packs up. Big Jimmy comes out of the kitchen.

"See if the cable's loose," he says to me.

"What cable?"

"The cable's underneath that shelf, wanker!" He points to the shelf where the sodas are stacked. (I told him that in England we don't usually refer to women as wankers. He said he didn't regard any of us as women.)

I bend down and look underneath the shelf. There are masses of wires.

"I'm not touching anything," I tell him.

"Me neither." Carole backs away.

"If you know so much about cables you bloody go down there," I say to him.

"What you think? I'm cooking. It's very hygienic I go down on the floor."

"You're scared!" says Carole.

"Yeah, you get down there you big macho Brazilian!"

"Stupid bastards," he says. "I don't care. You can't make tea; you lose the tips."

"Scaredy cat," we cry after him.

We call Nicky up at home.

"It better be an emergency," she shouts at the other end. *EastEnders* is on."

"The cappuccino machine's busted."

"Call up the repair guy. Jimmy will give you the number. Tell him he has to fix it tonight. It's Saturday tomorrow and if we ain't got hot water tell him . . . if there's any aggro tell him he can deal with me!"

Nicky gets a bit carried away when watching *EastEnders,* as if she's one of the characters. (It was partly due to her that the BBC's most popular soap is still shown on cable TV in New York—she organised a fund-raiser to save it.)

We call the repairman, who promises to send someone as soon as possible. At ten o'clock, the restaurant is empty. Big Jimmy is doing the kitchen bank and everything has been cleaned up. A short muscular man carrying a black bag comes in. He beams at us, saying: "You call-a me. I come-a fix the machine-o." He is very handsome, with black curly hair and lively brown eyes.

Big Jimmy swaggers out of the kitchen. "Over there," he says, pointing to the cappuccino machine. There's no hello or anything.

"We'll show him," Carole says and shoos Big Jimmy back to the kitchen.

"Carole, I'll show him. I speak Italian."

"Parla italiano?" The cappuccino man smiles and puts his hand on my shoulder.

"Cable-o," I say with an Italian accent. I point under the sodas.

The cappuccino man takes a torch from his bag and drops to his knees. He crawls

Deepak Verma, Sanjay from EastEnders, the most watched British television soap. From left to right he is with Carole, Anita and Nicky.

under the machine. His jeans arch, exposing the curve of his buttocks. Carole mouths a silent "cor."

He bangs something, and his cheeks vibrate.

"Would you like me to hold your torch?" I shout down to him. The cappuccino man comes up on his knees.

"Okay?" he asks smiling.

"Si si," I say. He goes back down.

"It might be easier if you take your trousers off," says Carole.

"I can lie underneath you," I call to him. "It will give you more leverage."

The cappuccino man's dark head pops up again. He smiles when he sees us laughing. The sound of laughter draws the big bastard out of the kitchen.

"What's going on? Nicky will be very angry if this doesn't work." Big Jimmy glowers at the cappuccino man. "She'll be mad as hell, mate."

"All right, all right. What do you think he's doing?"

"Yeah, mind your own business. Let him get on with it."

Big Jimmy goes back to the kitchen. The Italian man pokes his tongue out at him. We laugh extra loudly.

He gets back down on the floor, crouching even lower. His legs are bent like a frog. I take a pea off a dirty plate in the bus tray and drop it above his exposed cheeks.

The cappuccino man gives a yell and comes up again. Carole pretends to be organizing the cups. I wipe the cake stands. He reaches down into his trousers and pulls out the pea. He looks around and then up at the ceiling. We explode into laughter. His face registers delight when he realizes it came from us. He shakes a finger at us, before getting back under the shelf.

Suddenly, the light comes on and the cappuccino machine whirrs back into action. We clap and cheer. He comes back up and kisses us both on the cheek. I make the mistake of looking into his eyes. They widen as if I had just told him I loved him.

"Ginger beer?" I say.

He looks uncomprehending.

"Never mind her. She's a frustrated old bag," says Carole. "Coke? You want Coke?"

"Si," he says. He puts his torch back in his bag, and Carole hands him a cold Coke. We get our coats and make our way merrily to the door.

"Night, Big Jimmy," Carole and I call out.

"Night, Big Jimmy," the cappuccino man mimics.

Big Jimmy growls something back. We all break into laughter. The cappuccino man is in a real gay mood. He kisses our hands before climbing into his van.

"Come on then," I say to Carole. "Let's go and drink the wine."

"No thanks, I'm going home."

"Carole? Come on. I don't want to be on my own. Please?"

"You're not on you own. You've got mice!"

Carole walks off down the block.

"Bitch!" I yell after her.

I start walking to the subway. A horn honks. Driving alongside me is the cappuccino man. "You wanna ride?"

"Yes!" I climb into the van.

I tell him I live uptown. He reverses the van back past Tea & Sympathy to turn around. Big Jimmy is locking the gates. He looks up just as the van is about to turn. He sees me smiling through the window and does a double take. He literally stops in his tracks. As we speed off uptown, I blow him a kiss through the window.

Postscript: The cappuccino man managed to plug the holes with steel wool. His name was Mario and he came from a small village in Sicily. I never saw a mouse in that apartment again. Lindsay was surprisingly reticent about her night with the bacon man. He didn't show up the following Friday, however, with his weekly delivery. Nicky got herself into quite a state and banned us girls from courting the tradesmen.

Yorkshire Pudding

*T*he original Yorkshire pudding was cooked whole, cut up into squares, and served with gravy. It was eaten before the meat in order to fill you up. Today it is more like a popover and it is usually cooked in individual round muffin tins and served as an accompaniment to roast beef. The pudding should be light, crispy, and slightly soft in the middle. At the restaurant, we serve it with roast beef, lamb, or even chicken.

SERVES 6–8

PREPARATION TIME: 40 minutes

2 cups sifted all-purpose flour
1/2 teaspoon salt
4 eggs
2 cups whole milk
Vegetable oil

+ Preheat the oven to 425°F.
+ In a bowl, sift the flour and the salt.
+ Drop the eggs into the center of the flour mixture along with enough milk to form a smooth paste. Beat well with a whisk and gradually beat in the remaining milk. Cover and let rest in a cool place for 1 hour.
+ Coat the cups of a muffin tin, or coat an 11 x 7-inch baking pan with oil and heat until smoking hot.
+ Quickly pour in the batter, filling the cups about three-fourths full, and bake on a high rack until well risen: about 25–40 minutes, depending on how hot your oven is running. Do not open the oven while baking; otherwise the puddings will sink and will not rise again.
+ Serve hot.

Toad in the Hole

*I*n America this is known as "pig in a blanket," but in England this is a real "school dinner" meal. At boarding school ours was very stodgy and thick, more like pigs in a mattress. I like it that way but I also like the correct way, which is light and fluffy, with a little stodginess in the middle but crunchy on the outside.

6–8 sausages
4 tablespoons vegetable oil
1 recipe Yorkshire Pudding batter (page 72)

+ Preheat the oven to 375°F.
+ Pour the oil into a small roasting pan or ovenproof dish. Add the sausages and coat them with the oil.
+ Bake the sausages for 10–15 minutes, until they begin to brown and the oil is really hot.
+ Give the pudding batter a stir and pour it over the sausages. Bake for 30–40 minutes, or until risen and crisp around the edges.

Summer Pudding

*P*uddings in America are soft, mousse-like affairs. In England, pudding means any kind of dessert. At school, we would call it "afters" or "seconds." This is the easiest pudding to make, but people think you are a creative genius, because it looks like a lot of work has gone into it. Use a smooth round bowl so it will come out in a nice dome shape, then sprinkle a few fresh berries around the dish and plop a sprig of mint on top. I love it with a dollop of clotted cream or slightly whipped heavy cream.

SERVES 6–8

2 lbs. fresh berries (strawberries, raspberries,
*   and blueberries)*
1/2 cup sugar
Juice of 1 lemon
8–10 slices white bread
Whole berries for garnish
Mint sprig for garnish (optional)
Clotted cream or heavy cream (optional)

- Simmer the fruit with the sugar and lemon juice for 5 minutes, until the fruit has softened. Taste and add more sugar if necessary.
- Remove the crusts from the bread and line a dessert bowl with the slices, reserving enough bread to cover the top of the fruit.
- Fill the bread-lined bowl with the fruit and then cover with the remaining bread slices.
- Cover the bowl with a plate that fits inside of the bowl, so it sits directly on top of the pudding. Put something heavy on top to weight it down, and chill overnight.
- When ready to serve, place a large plate upside down on top of the pudding and flip over the pudding with the plate. The pudding should come out whole. (If the pudding doesn't come out whole, just serve it in individual serving dishes and garnish as below.)

• Garnish with some fresh berries and a sprig of mint. Serve with clotted cream, or fresh heavy cream, poured or whipped.

Flapjacks

Not to be confused with American flapjacks, these are very sweet and sticky and are fantastic for kids to make. Some recipes call for flour, but we make them without because when I was a child this is how my mother made them with me. When you serve them, do not stack them on top of each other, as they will stick together. If you are storing them, put waxed paper between the layers.

MAKES ABOUT 20 SQUARES
PREPARATION TIME: 20 minutes

3/4 cup (1 1/2 sticks) butter
1/4 cup Tate & Lyle golden syrup
1 cup light brown sugar
2 1/2 cups instant oatmeal
1/2 cup shredded coconut (supermarket variety)

• Preheat the oven to 350°F.
• Heat the butter and syrup together in a large pan until the butter has melted. Remove from the heat and stir in the remaining ingredients.
• Turn the batter onto a greased nonstick 7 x 11-inch tin and spread evenly. Bake for 15 minutes.
• Cool slightly and then cut into squares or fingers, if you prefer. Mark out and cut the cookies before they cool; otherwise, it is too difficult to cut them. If it does go too cold, you can always return it to the oven for 1 minute to soften.

Shortbread

Shortbread has nothing to do with bread; it is a biscuit or cookie that is most commonly associated with Scotland. Store-bought brands come in many shapes and sizes, usually in a tartan box or tin. I have made mine round, but you may use any size or shape cookie cutter that you wish. This is another great recipe to make with the kids.

MAKES ABOUT 8 BISCUITS

PREPARATION TIME: 45–55 minutes

1/2 cup (1 stick) butter, softened
1/4 cup sugar
1 1/2 cups sifted all-purpose-flour
Sugar for dusting

- Preheat the oven to 300°F.
- Lightly grease a baking tray.
- Beat the butter until soft.
- Add the sugar followed by the sifted flour and mix all the ingredients with your hands to form a stiff dough.
- Transfer the dough to a lightly sugared surface. Gently but quickly roll it out to a 1/8-inch thickness. Using a 3-inch fluted cookie cutter, cut out the biscuits, then prick all over with a fork.
- Arrange the cutout biscuits on the baking tray and bake on an upper rack for 30–40 minutes. They should be pale on top and slightly brown on the bottom.
- Remove the biscuits from the oven. Sprinkle with a little sugar, then cool on a wire rack.
- Store in an airtight container to keep the biscuits crisp. They will last 3–4 days.

Swiss Roll

Why is this called Swiss Roll? I have no idea. This is a fat-free sponge cake mixture, so no butter or margarine. You may substitute half of the flour with cocoa powder to make a chocolate Swiss Roll and instead of jam, use some of the butter cream (see page 58).

SERVES ABOUT 8–10

PREPARATION TIME: 45 minutes

3 eggs
1/3 cup plus 3 tablespoons sugar
3/4 cup sifted all-purpose flour
Wax paper
Sugar for dusting
6–8 tablespoons raspberry jam, warmed

- Preheat the oven to 400°F.
- Whisk the eggs and sugar until the whisk leaves a trail, then gently fold in the flour.
- Turn the mixture onto a paper-lined and greased 8 x 12-inch baking tray. Bake for 10–12 minutes, or until pale and golden and springy to the touch.
- On a slightly damp cloth, place a sheet of the wax paper and sprinkle it with sugar.
- Turn the sponge out, cake side down, onto the sugared paper, then remove the paper from the top of the sponge.
- Gently spread the sponge evenly with the jam.
- Carefully roll up the sponge from the short edge, using the cloth to help you.
- Let cool and then sprinkle with sugar.
- Trim off the edges and discard. Cut into slices and serve.

Iced Tea

*T*o make fantastic iced tea you need to make it quite strong. For better results use a flavored loose tea such as black currant, apricot, or mango, which are particular favorites. You can make a large batch and keep it in the refrigerator. It will last several days.

SERVES 6

PREPARATION TIME: 30 minutes

You will need:
6 heaping tablespoons loose tea per pot
1 large teapot
Fresh boiling water
1 tea strainer
1 large heatproof pitcher
Sugar (optional)

• Heat the pot by swirling a little boiling water in it.
• Spoon the tea into the teapot and cover with boiling water. Let it stand for a good 5 minutes.
• Give the tea a stir, then strain it into the pitcher.
• Refill the pot with more boiling water and the same tea leaves and again let stand for 5 minutes before straining it into the pitcher. This will give you approximately 10 glasses of tea with ice.
• If you are making a lot of tea, repeat the process and keep adding it to the pitcher, then chill.
• It is quite difficult to dissolve sugar in iced tea. A good tip is to mix some sugar with a little water and heat until the sugar dissolves. You may serve this on the side for those who like their iced tea sweet.

If you wish to serve the tea immediately: Cool it down by filling a zip-lock bag with ice and placing the bag in the hot tea until the ice cubes have melted. This will cool the tea without diluting the taste. Repeat until the tea is cold.

Another great idea for serving the tea: Fill some ice trays with the tea mixture. When ready to serve, fill the glass with the tea ice cubes and the iced tea. As the cubes melt, they will not weaken the tea.

If you wish to have something a little more exotic: You may add a little fresh fruit or mint sprigs to the tea. For example, if you use a peach tea, a couple of slices of fresh peaches added to the glass give it that little bit of extra flavor. Also, slices of mango in mango tea tastes luscious.

A watercolor given to Nicky done by Cathy Yarrow,
a waitress who left the restaurant.

CHAPTER FIVE

Tea, Sympathy . . .
and Comfort Food

One winter's day, a gaunt man with black hair and glasses walked into the restaurant and sat down at table nine. Without meeting my eyes, he picked up the menu I put on his table and quickly ordered the macaroni cheese, with a strong cup of tea. He looked familiar, and I thought I recognized his Irish lilt. But as he sat there for what must have been an hour, slowly picking his way through the large dish, I wasn't sure if I'd served him before.

"Is everything OK?" I asked.

He finally looked up at me and started to cry. He had not taken off his thick duffel coat and his glasses quickly steamed over. I could not mistake the tears that rushed down his cheeks.

"I'm sorry," I said. "I didn't mean to upset you."

"Don't worry, it's not your fault," he said, the tears still running down his face. "I've just found out that I've got the Dreaded."

"The Dreaded?" I was standing behind the cake counter. I leaned toward him because he was speaking softly.

"AIDS," he whispered. "I've just found out that I've got AIDS." His eyes flooded with tears and he looked back down at his macaroni cheese dish. I didn't know what to say so I went and made us a pot of tea.

One of my earliest memories in the restaurant, and I'm ashamed to describe it, was just having cleared someone's table and then hearing that the person had AIDS. I felt really nervous and snuck away to the bathroom to wash my hands. Now AIDS was an everyday part of my life. You couldn't work in Greenwich Village without it being so; we had lost so many customers.

One of them, Peter, was a regular customer who'd been coming since we opened. He was also a neighbor and owned a shop across the street. He'd had AIDS for a long time and his deterioration was slow. He'd undergone a lot of surgery, for failing eyes and numerous other problems. Later his hearing went and we'd have to shout. Then, often, he got quite bad-tempered, although no one ever took offense. Suzy would sit and share a cigarette with him, which I think he liked, and Nicky regarded him as a friend. He must have felt the same because when he passed away, he left a budget in his will to hold his memorial at Tea & Sympathy. He wanted champagne, finger sandwiches, and scones. We closed the restaurant and all his family and friends crammed inside. Nicky was so upset that she stayed in her office. Peter was the first regular we'd lost who had also been a friend.

From left to right: Sophie, George and Nadia. Nadia is part of the T&S family. In the early days, she brought hordes of friends nearly every day.

For some customers who contracted AIDS, our food was the only food they could stomach. And when their taste buds let them down they could still sit and have a cigarette and a cup of tea. They felt relaxed and accepted—no one was going to sit and stare at them.

I'd often heard British food dismissed as "mere comfort food," without really understanding what the phrase meant. I gradually found out what it meant to different people, and not just to those suffering from AIDS. And I found out what a well-run restaurant could mean to its customers. There was one couple who had a ritual of celebrating the birth of each child with a trip to us. They came directly from the maternity ward at St. Vincent's Hospital, just a few blocks down on Greenwich Avenue. The last time I saw them they'd just had their fourth child. The tiny newborn boy was perched in his car seat on top of the next table. The wife said the teashop was like the "light at the end of a tunnel": No matter how painful labor was, she knew she'd eventually make it here for a bread and butter pudding and a cup of tea.

Constables from the British Cleveland police: They collected $25,000 in plastic buckets on the streets of Cleveland, UK, and then flew to New York to give it to the NYPD 6th Precinct after September 11. We all toasted them with tea and biscuits.

♦ ♦ ♦

For Robert, Tea & Sympathy almost became home. One day he was walking along Greenwich Avenue, fretting about how he couldn't get a decent cup of tea in New York. He'd just returned from working in London, where he'd lived with an English family. He'd got used to sitting at their round kitchen table, drinking cups of tea. It was at that moment that he passed T&S: The door was wide open; Nicky's friend Helen was finishing up stenciling the floors with teacups and saucers; he saw the little tables in their floral Laura Ashley cloths and beyond the Welsh dresser with its beautiful assortment of china. It reminded him of the little teashops he'd encountered in the English countryside. The next day he came for lunch. He sat at table five and ordered finger sandwiches and Assam tea. Before long he was eating here every day.

At first Robert brought in only his newspaper, then his books, and finally his work. One day he said he wanted to spend all day in the restaurant. He gave each of us a very generous tip and stayed for breakfast, lunch, and through to supper. (This was in the early days before we were busy.) As an anglophile bachelor, he'd found a replacement English family bang in the middle of New York.

◆ ◆ ◆

Smitty was another regular who lived in the neighborhood. He was an old man who every now and then hobbled over for scones and coffee. If we saw him coming, one of us would run out and help him cross Greenwich Avenue. He'd sit on table five with his cane resting against the window. He liked to drink his coffee and look out of the window. He never passed up the opportunity for a chance to flirt, and every time we went to his table, or a single woman chanced to sit on table six, his eyes lit up. He was a lovely man and even though he was in his eighties, he had the cheeky grin of a nineteen-year-old. Nicky only ever charged him for his coffee. When he was ready to go, her husband, Sean, walked him home. Later Smitty got an electric-powered wheelchair, and he'd arrive at the door as frisky and debonair as a gentleman racer from the 1930s.

◆ ◆ ◆

Comfort food and the comfort of tea worked in many mysterious ways. Once I watched a fascinating little scene unroll before my eyes. It began with a mother and son sitting on table eight. The mother was obviously upset but was trying to keep calm while she told her son what a ridiculous idea it was for him to marry a girl whom he'd only just met. "Marriage is a serious commitment," she kept repeating, to which the son replied, "I know. That's why we want to do it."

Naughty Lindsay with Smitty.

After fifteen minutes the girlfriend eventually arrived. She was tall and pretty and somewhat flustered. The boyfriend stood up, smiling, when he saw her. Then I realized mother and prospective daughter-in-law were meeting for the first time. The girl bent over and shook hands, apologizing for her lateness.

Then the son asked the girl how she was and the mother listened, smiling politely. I could only imagine what she was feeling, to be introduced to a perfect stranger who is suddenly to be a part of your life. I took the opportunity to take their order, which was for three afternoon teas.

I couldn't help being nosy; the scenario fascinated me. After they'd got their food I started cleaning the cappuccino machine so I could continue to keep an eye on them. It was then that I discovered that afternoon tea was a perfect choice for an awkward situation, a great accompaniment to small talk. There's a ritual involved in tea. Generally one person does all the pouring, which in this case was the mother—it was her way of falling into a

Anita, actually working for a change, instead of reading her screenplays or doubled over laughing behind the cake counter or hiding in the bathroom with a hangover.

role that made it all easier. They compared notes on how they liked their teas; both mother and daughter-in-law liked their Typhoo strong.

"I haven't got a chance," the son said when he heard this. The two women burst out laughing and I felt a surge of relief—maybe everything was going to be all right after all. Everyone relaxed, and in between comments on the finger sandwiches and how clotted cream ought to be illegal, the door gradually opened to a discussion about the impending marriage. At this point I put an end to my eavesdropping. The cappuccino machine was so clean it looked brand new.

◆ ◆ ◆

Thinking back, there's quite a romantic tradition at T&S. More than one waitress has eloped with a customer never to be seen again. At one point Nicky considered employing married women only.

But Nicky can't complain: Tea & Sympathy was where she met Sean. A friend of Sean's was sitting on table nine having a cup of tea with a mate when he decided to have a taste

Tea & Sympathy

Nicky and Sean on their way to the Plaza to celebrate the digitally remastered release of My Fair Lady.

of his friend's custard. With his teaspoon, he helped himself only to find Nicky glowering over him.

"Oy!" she scolded. "Get your hands off his custard."

"I just wanted to see whether it was Bird's," Sean's friend said, referring to Britain's most popular custard mix.

Nicky looked even angrier. "Of course it's frigging Bird's," she screamed.

When Sean heard this story, he said to his mate, "I've got to meet this woman." Two years later they were married in Vegas in a drive-in ceremony.

♦ ♦ ♦

Another customer, Sarah, a writer and psychotherapist, always orders scones with chamomile tea. Sometimes, in between bites of scone, she closes her eyes. One day I was cleaning the next table when I heard this deep, drawn-out grunting sound. I looked up and saw Sarah sitting there with her eyes shut.

"Are you all right Sarah?" I asked, quickly.

She opened her eyes. "I'm just doing Pranyama," she said. "I don't know if you're aware, but this is a very spiritual place."

The last time Sarah was in, Nicky was in an uproar about a broken teapot. Sarah tapped her on the arm before leaving and said, "I really think you should chant and write poetry."

Nicky looked at her. "Bollocks," she said.

♦ ♦ ♦

Once, I'd just put the monkey teapot in front of a woman when she showed me a brown paper bag and took out a little purple teddy.

"Today's the day, so I came here," she said. I nodded as if I understood, but it was only when I was walking back to the podium that I remembered: It was the second anniversary of the death of Lady Di.

Over the years Diana had become an integral part of life at Tea & Sympathy. There was always some snippet of gossip in the English tabloids that Nicky bought daily. Following the royals was a bit like watching the cockney soap opera *EastEnders:* It was both entertaining and it linked us with home.

Nicky was especially fond of Di. She took the bulimia, the divorce and the abuses of her private life to heart. When the *Panorama* interview came out in England, Nicky finagled for it to be flown over seventy-two hours before it was shown on American television. She fixed up a video player in the restaurant and showed it on a loop for the next three days. Customers turned their chairs to face the TV. When Diana spoke the words "There were three of us in this marriage," it was so quiet you could have heard a pin drop.

When she died, early Sunday morning on August 31, 1997, I was on holiday in Greece and Nicky was in England. Sean opened early because he knew we'd be mobbed. Tea & Sympathy had become the hub for New York's English diaspora. It was a gathering place, so much so that if you met a British person, it was very rare if they hadn't been to T&S, or at least heard of it. On Diana's death, Brits, Americans and people of all nationalities arrived at Tea & Sympathy to mourn. Some sat crying, while others drank their tea in silence. Suzy was working that day and said she spent all day making pots of tea and giving hugs. Numerous TV crews arrived to interview customers.

Nicky called Sean every half hour, sobbing. Everyone was in shock. They needed understanding and comfort, and Tea & Sympathy gave them both.

British makeup artist Mark Hayles, another regular from the very beginning.

♦ ♦ ♦

One day a regular customer, Archie, told me how he'd been attending his weekly Weight Watchers motivational meeting when the conversation had turned to Tea & Sympathy. It was actually the group leader who brought it up, saying it was a great place to go and have a calm moment and a respectable cup of tea. The rest of the group began discussing their own Tea & Sympathy favorites. Archie, with more than a tinge of guilt, admitted his passion for the treacle pudding and custard. The group leader replied that it was indeed possible to enjoy Tea & Sympathy in the true spirit of Weight Watchers.

"If you are going to have the treacle pudding and custard," she said, "then make sure you enjoy every bite. Really taste it, and let it be a profoundly wonderful experience."

Portrait of Nicky and Rosie
by Don Perlis.

Macaroni Cheese/Cauliflower Cheese

This dish may be served on its own or as a side dish. I like to substitute cauliflower for the traditional macaroni, which is so delicious that even my husband loves it, and he does not eat vegetables.

SERVES 4–6

PREPARATION TIME: 45 minutes

1 large cauliflower, broken into large florets
1/4 cup (1/2 stick) butter
1 onion, peeled and finely chopped
3 slices bacon (optional)
3 slightly heaping tablespoons all-purpose flour
2 cups milk
2 cups grated sharp Cheddar cheese*
A pinch of English mustard powder (optional)
Salt and pepper

*You can use any cheese you like; the stronger the cheese the better.

- Preheat the broiler.
- Cook the cauliflower in lightly salted water until tender. Drain it and arrange in an ovenproof baking dish.
- Melt the butter and sauté the onion and bacon, if using, until the onion is soft and the bacon is cooked.
- Using a slotted spoon, spoon the onion and bacon over the cauliflower so that the butter remains in the pan.
- Over medium heat, add the flour to the butter in the pan and stir for 1 minute.
- Remove the pan from the heat and slowly add the milk, a little at a time, stirring constantly until the mixture thickens.

- Return the pan to the heat and bring to a boil, stirring constantly. Reduce the heat and simmer, stirring occasionally, for 4–5 minutes. You may need to add a little more milk.
- Preheat the broiler.
- Remove the pan from the heat and stir in 1 3/4 cups of the cheese and all of the mustard powder, if using. The mixture should have a nice thick and creamy consistency.
- Add salt and pepper to taste—not too much salt as the cheese will be quite salty.
- Pour the cheese sauce over the cauliflower and sprinkle it with the remaining cheese. Place the dish under the broiler and cook until the top starts to go golden brown and bubbles.

Chicken Soup

*T*his is the best chicken soup you will ever have and it is great for freezing. The parsnips give the soup a delicious sweetness, and everyone knows how good chicken soup is for you, whether you are sick or not. This soup is a meal in itself; it is so packed with vegetables that it is almost like chicken stew.

SERVES 8–12

PREPARATION TIME: 2 1/2 hours

2 large onions, peeled and chopped
1 whole chicken
6 stalks celery, washed and chopped
4 bay leaves
2 tablespoons herbes de Provence or chopped fresh herbs
2 large potatoes, peeled and chopped into bite-sized pieces
6 medium carrots, peeled and chopped

2 large white or yellow turnips, peeled and chopped
4 medium parsnips, peeled and chopped
1 box tiny sweet frozen peas
Salt and pepper

+ In a stockpot, combine the onions, chicken, celery, bay leaves, and herbs. Add enough cold water to cover the chicken and bring to a boil. Reduce the heat and simmer for approximately 1 hour, depending on the size of the chicken, until the chicken is soft enough to easily come off the bone.
+ When the chicken is cooked, remove it from the pan and let it cool.
+ While the chicken is cooling, simmer the potatoes, carrots, turnips, and parsnips in the stock over medium heat until the vegetables are cooked, about 30 minutes. Add the peas for the last 5 minutes of cooking time.
+ Add salt and pepper to taste, then add the chicken once you have taken it off the bone.

Cornish Pasty

*F*or hundreds of years the Cornish pasty or variations of it has been eaten as a working man's midday meal—hot or cold, with or without a side of salad, coleslaw, or beans, it is delicious and convenient. It is an excellent dish for lunch or supper and is great for picnics or made in miniature for cocktail parties. At the restaurant, we serve this with either a green salad or mashed potato and baked beans.

SERVES 6–8
PREPARATION TIME: about 2 1/2 hours

1 tablespoon olive oil
2 medium onions, peeled and diced
2 small carrots, peeled and finely diced

2 lbs. ground lamb (or beef, if preferred)

3 medium potatoes, peeled and finely diced

1 teaspoon herbes de Provence *or chopped mixed herbs*

2 tablespoons Worcestershire sauce

2 pinches English mustard powder (optional)

1 egg

Salt and pepper

Double recipe of Savoury Suet Pastry (page 110)

- To prepare the filling: Sauté the onions in the oil until they are soft.
- Add the lamb and cook for 15 minutes. Add the *herbes de Provence,* Worcestershire sauce and mustard. Cook on a low heat, stirring occasionally, for 1 hour and 40 minutes. Add the carrots for the last 5 minutes of cooking, stirring constantly.
- Cook the potatoes in boiling salted water until they are tender.
  Season the lamb mixture with salt and pepper to taste and add the cooked potatoes.
- Preheat the oven to 350°F.
- To prepare the pastry: Roll out the pastry to a thickness of 1/4 inch and cut into rounds about 6 inches across.
- Divide the filling equally among the pastry rounds. Crimp the edges firmly together and make a small slit in the top to allow the steam to escape.
- Brush with beaten egg and bake 45–60 minutes, until golden brown.

Mashed Potato

Mashed potato is so versatile. It is great served as a side dish or as a substitute for pie-crust as in our Shepherd's Pie (see page 37). In Ireland, they add fresh scallions; this is known as colcannon, which is traditionally served on Halloween. You may also add more butter or milk to this recipe if you like it really creamy, but if you are topping a pie with it, don't let it get too sloppy, otherwise it will get runny when placed in the oven.

SERVES 2–3 (For a pie that serves 6–8, double this recipe.)
PREPARATION TIME: 30 minutes

3 lbs. potatoes, peeled
    (Idaho potatoes are ideal.)
1/2 cup (1 stick) butter
Whole milk
Salt and pepper to taste

- Coarsely chop the potatoes and boil in lightly salted water for 20–25 minutes, until soft.
- Drain them well and then mash the potatoes, stir in the butter and add the milk little by little until you reach your desired consistency.
- Add salt and pepper to taste.

Very Rich Bread & Butter Pudding

*B*read and Butter pudding, also known as nursery pudding, dates back to the eighteenth century. It is really custard baked with bread. This version is very rich and is best served warm. It is best made with bread that is a day or two old; you should always use good-quality bread, not processed bread.

SERVES 4–6
PREPARATION TIME: 1 1/2 hours

For the pudding:
1 loaf* white bread, 1 or 2 days old, sliced.
1 cup raisins—light, dark, or mixed
1/4 cup sugar
6 tablespoons dark rum (optional)

(*Whole loaves are better than presliced.)

- Preheat the oven to 350°F.
- Trim the crusts from the bread and butter most of the slices apart from a few, which should be left unbuttered for the top layer.
- Line a 3-inch-deep 8 x 8-inch dish with the buttered bread, buttered side up, and sprinkle with a little sugar and raisins.
- Continue to layer the dish with the bread, sugar and raisins until almost full, leaving space for 1 more layer of unbuttered bread.

For the custard:
3/4 cup heavy cream
1 cup whole milk
1/4 cup plus 1 tablespoon granulated sugar

1/2 teaspoon pure vanilla extract

4 egg yolks

1 cup dark brown sugar

- To prepare the custard: Heat the cream, milk, sugar, and vanilla until hot but not boiling.
- Remove the pan from the heat and whisk the egg yolks into the hot milk, then add rum if desired.
- Cut the remaining unbuttered bread into triangles. Place the bread triangles, overlapping slightly, on top of the pudding.
- Pour the custard mixture evenly over the top.
- Sprinkle the top evenly with the dark brown sugar and cover with foil.
- Place the dish in a large roasting pan and place it in the oven. Fill the roasting pan with enough boiling water to reach two thirds of the way up the side of the pudding dish. Bake for about 40 minutes.
- Remove the foil and bake for another 10 minutes to crisp the top.

CHAPTER SIX

Nicky's Rules

Amonth after Bryan Miller gave us our rave review in *The New York Times,* Nicky received an invitation to attend a cocktail party benefit for the Royal Ballet—quite an honour for the owner of a little teashop. The benefit was on the same day that Nicky was flying to England. She was planning to attend a food trade show and to get bolts of fabric at Laura Ashley to replace our already scuffed tablecloths. Before she left she gave me the invitation and told me to go and take her place. I was excited; I imagined a glamorous event packed with famous people. It was being held in a fancy hotel uptown and I took along an American friend from acting class who'd been a ballet dancer. We entered the reception and I handed my invitation to a youngish dancer-type woman. Within moments I was whisked away and introduced to an attractive elderly couple . . . as Ms. Nicola Perry.

"We've heard delightful things about your restaurant," the man said, shaking my hand. "That's next on our agenda of downtown trips."

They were both beaming, genuinely thrilled to meet me. I hadn't the heart to tell them

Nicky and her dog, the beautiful Rosie Lee (Cockney slang for Cuppa Tea). Photograph by Charles Harris for Vogue magazine

that I was only a waitress—and not a particularly competent one at that. Instead I straightened up, gave them a cheeky smile, and said, "Fab! Let me know when you're coming. I'll make sure my girls give you the right royal treatment." Needless to say, they were ecstatic.

Well, it went on and on with me being introduced as Nicola Perry. Everyone was eager to shake my hand. As there wasn't one celebrity I recognized, I came to the conclusion that I was probably the most famous person there. Everyone seemed to have heard of Tea & Sympathy and the name was eliciting the same note of delighted surprise from them all: "Oh, Tea & Sympathy? How wonderful! It's a pleasure to meet you Nicola."

Everyone wanted to discuss their favorite restaurant, and did I know so and so who owned blah blah? I said "yes" to everything because Nicky knows masses of restaurants and their owners, past and present. I was just glad that no one tried to talk about ballet. My downfall came a little later: I was the center of a small group of which I was the youngest by about thirty years. I had a glass of champagne in each hand, and was drinking from both, when a woman asked, "When did you open your restaurant?"

"When did I open?" I repeated. It was just a question of subtracting months from the present, but my mind went blank. They looked at me expectantly, but I just couldn't remember. A date kept popping into my head: It was 1066, the Battle of Hastings. "Some time now, but, er, not that long ago," I ended up saying. I made my getaway soon after. Interestingly, my friend never remarked on my new identity.

When Nicky returned from England, I told her all about the party and how I'd impersonated her. She laughed and promised me that if anyone from the cocktail party showed up we could swap places.

But the very fact that she had received the invitation confirmed what Nicky already suspected, which was that Tea & Sympathy was being looked upon as the unofficial British embassy.

Nicky began her tea career at fourteen, serving tea, sandwiches, and Kit Kat bars to stodgy brokers at the London Stock Exchange. Wearing skintight jeans and scarlet painted nails, she'd totter around on her ten-inch polka dot platforms pushing a tea trolley. Apparently she was a vision compared to the old dears who usually worked there, with their missing teeth and dinner-lady overalls. At sixteen she failed her O levels and was flung out of boarding ballet school. She spent the next few years living with Glen Tillbrook and Jools Holland of Squeeze and hanging out with Boy George. Then at twenty-one she followed her dreams to New York. By twenty-three she'd decided she wanted her own teashop: at that time it was impossible to buy a really good cup of tea in the city; American cafés were still

using an inferior tea bag and the tepid water from the coffee machines. For the next eight years Nicky carried around the concept for her teashop-cum-restaurant. She envisioned it right down to the tablecloths. After a decade of waitressing, she found the little space on Greenwich Avenue. She opened Tea & Sympathy on the night before Christmas Eve in 1990.

In the early days our best table, table one, was reserved for staff. A constant stream of Nicky's friends would sit for hours drinking tea and eating. There were two waitresses on each shift so generally you'd take it in turns to serve, while the other sat and read *Hello* magazine and drank her tea. Sometimes I'd read a novel and be so engrossed in it that I'd forget where I was. At the busiest times there might be only four or five tables occupied, and conversations would spring up between them. The regulars all knew each other. We were like an

Erin O'Connor, British fashion model and Tea & Sympathy regular. Photograph by Arthur Elgore for British Vogue magazine.

Fashion photographer Steve Hiett with one of his models, in a snapshot by fashion photographer Arthur Elgore.

oddball extended family. Nicky still refers to these regulars as "our bread and butter," because without them we wouldn't have lasted even long enough to receive our breakthrough reviews.

Once the restaurant became exposed to the world outside the Village, we soon became busy: Customers from as far away as Korea came clutching magazines with reviews about us; the number of regulars tripled; and it became a popular haunt for the fashion world. British supermodels Kate Moss and Naomi Campbell made it their home away from home. (Naomi became responsible for bringing tea strainers over from England.) They'd sit there tucking into treacle pudding and custard and reading the British newspapers. I remember once overhearing Kate Moss reading something about Naomi having her feet done, and saying, "Oh! Me Mum told me she'd 'ad 'em done!"

Later T&S was the backdrop for Kate Moss's romance with Johnny Depp. They sat at table one—the staff had been chased off it by now—and looked adoringly into each other's eyes. Johnny Depp could barely take his hands off her face, except of course when his treacle pudding arrived. (They nearly missed a flight to LA waiting for treacle pudding and custard to go.)

Christy Turlington and Paulina were both early regulars, as were fashion photographers, actors and designers, including Rifat Ozbek, Anna Sui, Isaac Mizrahi and Helmut Lang. I served Helmut once, not knowing who he was, and got a bit chatty when I found out he was from Vienna, where my step-grandmother had

Nicky and Archie, from Flyleaf, who has been a regular since the beginning of time, and who designed all of the menus for the restaurant.

lived. I bored the designer pants off him talking about my childhood memories, before asking, "So how do you like New York?"

One day Arthur Miller came for dinner. I was so excited I treated him like a king. I had just plucked up the courage to speak to him when he gave me his credit card. I read the name and saw it wasn't Arthur Miller after all.

The lines at the weekend continued to grow until sometimes they went all the way down the block. Regulars were sent to Johnny's Bar and we'd call them when there was a table. The people waiting in line imagined they were jumping the queue.

Anna Sui, another fashion impresario who has been coming to Tea & Sympathy for ages.

At weekends there were now three of us per shift, not including Nicky. She refused to do the door because she'd get so stressed out that the vein above her temple would start to throb. We ended up keeping a list. For some reason we'd never write down names but identify customers by either physical descriptions or food preferences: "Tell the Two Fat Ladies to come in," "Table's ready for the twins!" (these were identical fifty-year-old twin brothers), "Get the Tattooed Lady," "Where's Scones Heated Up buggered off to?" "Table ten for Stilton Welsh Rarebit" (an old lady who ate this every Saturday for eight years), and so on. Even with a list, queue rage broke out over who was first: There were the shy ones who didn't dare speak out and the aggressive ones who pushed their way to the front. Tremendous dramas were enacted outside the door. I'd look out and see this endless line of people queuing for forty minutes in subzero conditions. The problem

Rifat Ozbek, British fashion designer, having his birthday with us.

Gilly, who met her husband at Tea & Sympathy, but alas has moved back to England.

was that no matter how busy we were, we still had only ten tables. Some customers spent hours drinking their tea or writing novels and once a group of architects took up four tables upon which they spread their plans. Nicky would fret and pace as she waited for a table whose occupants displayed no visible intent to leave. In turn we all became tense, because like Nicky we, too, depended on a constant turnover of customers to pay the rent.

Then one day Nicky posted a white laminated card on the outside door. In bold black ink were written Nicky's Rules.

"There," she said. "I've spelled it out. If anyone's got a problem they can piss off and go and eat in Benny's Burritos."

A huge weight had been lifted from her shoulders. The years of guilt, hostility, and bickering, and the hours consumed in patient explanations as to why a latecomer could not join his party, were neatly summarized. The six rules became tantamount to the Ten Commandments, only you really had to follow them. And under Nicky's Rules was written: "These rules apply to everybody." From now on everyone had to toe the line, celebrities, regulars, and newcomers alike.

Laura, left, and Tania, two Scottish waitresses who never failed to make us laugh.

1. Be pleasant to waitresses. Tea & Sympathy girls are always right.

What often happened was an irate customer invariably asked to speak to the boss. Now you could just wave rule number one in their face. I have to say though that when a customer was particularly vile and insistent, I'd say, "Well maybe if you speak to Nicky, the owner, she might make an exception." I'd watch their departing back with glee. A few minutes later I'd call Nicky.

"What did you tell the customer who wanted to sit down and wait for his friend?"

"What do you think I told him, I told him to naff right off! He asked me if I'd make an exception, the arrogant sod! He won't be coming back!"

2. No exceptions. You'll have to wait outside until your entire party is present. Latecomers will not be seated.

Rachael, our beautiful Liverpudlian waitress.

This is the rule that incurs the most hostility, and contains the most potential for confusion and absurdity. A typical scenario would be a customer coming in, sitting at a table, and ordering tea while waiting for someone to join them. It might be a good forty minutes before the friend arrives and skips ahead of the queue, then they'd both be there another forty minutes eating.

I used to let people in to wait, especially if Nicky had gone home or the restaurant was empty. I took a chance though, because we could fill up in a matter of minutes. And making exceptions caused no end of embarrassing scenes: "How come she's allowed to wait and I'm not?" or "Well I was allowed to wait the last time I was here!"

Sometimes a customer will pretend he or she is alone. A few minutes later the friend arrives. "I'm sorry," you say, "but your friend can't join you."

"My friend can't join me? But the restaurant's empty?"

Lovely Lynsay on the left, and Naughty Lindsay on the right, both waitresses.

Rachael, another much-missed waitress.

"I know, but you knew the rule before you sat down."

"Yes, but every table's free."

This is when you cross the line into absurdity. The next thing the smart aleck friend will go and sit on the next table and say something cute like "Am I allowed to sit here?"

Now, of course, they're taking up two tables instead of one. The rule is being turned against you. "Oh sit where you like," I end up saying huffily. I once tried to discuss this dilemma with Nicky but she kept repeating, "There are no exceptions. The rules are the rules."

3. Occasionally you may be asked to change tables so we can accommodate all of you.

This is a pretty straightforward rule, but implementing it can be an unpleasant chore. Basically two people are tucking into roast beef dinners on table two and a party of four arrives. We need to join up tables two and three to accommodate the four. The decision is made: Table two will have to be moved. We arrive at the table armed with *trapos* (rags) and two setups.

"If you don't mind we're going to move you to another table?" It's not really a question, we're already picking up their plates and drinks. Bewildered, and still chewing, they follow us to their new table.

"There! Now you're much nearer the air conditioner!"

4. There is an $8.50 minimum charge per person.

This is to eliminate the groups of customers of whom two might only want tap water. It really pertains to our size: People are always waiting, and financially we just haven't got the space for small checks. (My God, I'm beginning to sound like Nicky!)

5. If we don't need the table you may stay all day, but if people are waiting and you have finished your meal then it's time to naff off.

* Sorry but we are trying to make everyone happy. When we are busy there will be a time limit and you will be asked to leave. Nothing personal.

Lindsay once said to me she'd never been so embarrassed as when one busy Sunday Nicky had shouted across to her, "Table five! Get 'em out of here!" Lindsay looked over and saw two ninety-year-old ladies sitting sweetly behind an empty afternoon tea stand.

Waitresses: Claire on the left and Zandra on the right.

I find asking people to leave horribly embarrassing. Sometimes customers remain at their table even after they've paid. If this happens all the waitresses swoop down and bus the table. If that doesn't budge them Nicky sends you to get rid of them. I'll confess it now, because I don't work there anymore, but I devised a way around this awkward task: I simply pretended to have told them to get out. Under Nicky's apoplectic gaze, I'd go to the table and say something like "I know this sounds silly, but what day of the week is it?"

Nicky, observing the interaction and the bemused look on the customers' faces, was satisfied I'd delivered the message. And it often happened that the question triggered off an association with time, and they'd end up leaving anyway, or else they thought their waitress had a screw loose. I still wonder though how people can hang around with half an inch of cold tea in their cup and remain oblivious to the crowd waiting outside.

6. Out-of-town visitors please note that it is customary in New York City to tip. A good guide is to double the sales tax; however feel free to tip the girls more if you wish.

A lot of our customers are foreign tourists who don't know the rules over here. And if they've just arrived, Tea & Sympathy might only be the second restaurant they've eaten in and they've not got their head around the local customs. (Although this state of ignorance

COFFEE AND A KICK IN THE PANTS
(FORMERLY TEA AND SYMPATHY)

n.Chast

won't last long; an irate cabby or waiter will soon put you right).

Even Americans can ignore the rules though: Robert—preppy, polite, charming Robert—once chased an entire family down the street because the father had told the lovely Rachael he would not tip as a protest against our seating rule. Robert verbally assaulted him on the corner of Greenwich Avenue and Thirteenth Street and told him never to darken our doors again. It was so out of character, but I think it had been building up for years. Robert was one of our first customers and he'd been coming almost every day since we opened (except one week when he went to his father's funeral). He knew as much as we did about Tea & Sympathy, and when we were busy he stacked his dirty crockery and carried it to the bus tray. He identified so much with the waitresses that when the man stiffed us he took it as personally as if he himself had been stiffed.

♦ ♦ ♦

A couple of years ago a woman sitting at table five kept looking at her watch.

"She's waiting for someone," Nicky said suspiciously. She went up to the woman and told her she'd have to leave and come back when her friend arrived.

"I don't think you understand," the woman said. "I'm waiting for Monica Lewinsky."

"I'm sorry," Nicky told her. "But until she gets back from the dry cleaners, you'll have to wait outside."

The woman ended up waiting two and a half hours before Monica arrived.

Postscript: The six rules have now been incorporated into the menu. When I asked Nicky if it was really necessary, she said, "People are like little children, Anita. They like boundaries."

Sweet Pastry

*I*t is very important when making pastry that before rolling it out you chill it for at least half an hour—an hour or two is even better. When you roll it, try to handle it as little as possible.

4 cups sifted all-purpose flour
A pinch of salt
1 1/4 cups (2 1/2 sticks) butter
1/2 cup sugar
2 eggs

- Combine the flour and salt in a bowl and rub in the butter until the mixture resembles fine bread crumbs.
- In another bowl, beat the sugar and eggs until the sugar has dissolved.
- Make a well in the center of the flour and pour in the egg mixture; stir with a knife until you have a stiff dough.
- Roll the pastry into a ball and wrap in cling wrap; refrigerate for at least 1/2 hour before using.
- Take the pastry out of the refrigerator about 10 minutes before you use it, so that it doesn't crumble when you roll it.

Short Crust Pastry

YIELD: 1 PIE CRUST
PREPARATION TIME: 20 minutes

2 cups sifted all-purpose flour
1/4 cup (1/2 stick) butter
1/2 cup lard or solid shortening
5 1/2 tablespoons iced water
1 teaspoon salt

+ Sift the flour and salt into a bowl. Rub in the butter and shortening until the mixture resembles bread crumbs.
+ Make a well in the center of the mixture and gradually add the water.
+ Mix with a palette knife until you have a firm dough and all the crumbs in the bottom of the bowl have been incorporated. Then roll the pastry into a ball, making sure it all sticks together properly. Handle the pastry as little as possible.
+ Wrap the dough in cling wrap and refrigerate for at least a half hour before using.
+ Take the pastry out of the refrigerator about 10 minutes before you roll it, so that it doesn't crumble when you roll it.

TIPS
When rolling out pastry put plenty of flour on the surface and rolling pin to prevent sticking.
Roll as little as possible; the less you handle the pastry the better it will be.
When making savoury pies, brush the top with a little beaten egg before baking.
When using sweet pastry, brush with a little milk and sprinkle with sugar.

◆ Suet ◆

We do not use suet in the restaurant for two reasons: Suet is beef fat and in this day of vegetarianism, the dishes we can make without the suet tend to be just as good. In addition, most pastries and puddings made with suet are steamed and steaming takes much longer and takes up more time and space in the kitchen. However, you can get vegetable suet, which also provides the stodgy element required but doesn't have the richness of the beef suet.

If you cannot find Atora suet in your local gourmet store, your local butcher should be able to provide you with beef fat suet, which is basically a big block of fat. Make sure there is no meat attached to it; if there is, cut it off. The fat may seem very plasticky; if so, cut off anything that resembles cling wrap.

Grate in a food processor like grating cheese. Transfer the grated suet to a bowl and add a little bit of flour so that it doesn't stick together. For every pound of suet, add 2 tablespoons of flour. Use as needed.

If stored in the refrigerator the suet will keep for a few days.

Sweet Suet Pastry

2 cups sifted all-purpose flour
3/4 cup sugar
1 cup suet
1 tablespoon baking powder
3/4 cup whole milk

◆ Mix together the flour, sugar, suet and baking powder.
◆ Make a well in the center and stir in the milk. Mix well.

- Roll out two-thirds of the pastry and use it to line a well-buttered 1-quart pudding basin.
- Fill with desired filling, e.g., Sussex Pond Pudding (see page 111). Seal with the remainder of the pastry.
- Put a buttered piece of wax paper over the top, followed by pleated foil, and tie it with string tightly around the edges.
- Steam for 1 1/2–3 hours. Refer to page 112 for instructions.

Savoury Suet Pastry

For Savoury Pastry:
1 cup sifted all-purpose flour
1 tablespoon baking powder
1 1/2 teaspoons salt
1/2 cup suet
3/4 cup water

For the filling:
Savoury filling of choice, e.g., Steak & Kidney (see page 164),
    Steak & Guinness (see page 163)

- Mix together the dry ingredients and the suet.
- Make a well in the center and stir in the water.
- Roll out two-thirds of the pastry and use it to line a well-buttered 1-quart pudding basin.
- Fill with desired filling; seal with the remainder of the pastry.
- Put a buttered piece of wax paper over the top, followed by pleated aluminum foil, and tie it with string tightly around the edges.
- Steam for 1 1/2 to 2 hours. Refer to page 112 for instructions.

Sussex Pond Pudding

*U*nfortunately, we do not make this at our restaurant anymore, as we do not have the space in our tiny kitchen for pots to be simmering with water for two hours. I love the tangy lemon and caramel flavor from the brown sugar and the sticky texture of suet pastry, and the lemon ends up being all soft and mushy.

SERVES 4–6
PREPARATION TIME: 2–2 1/2 hours

Sweet Suet Pastry (page 109)

For the filling:
1 small lemon
1 1/4 cups raisins
1/2 cup (1 stick) butter
1 cup dark brown sugar

+ Line a well-buttered 1-quart pudding basin with 3/4 cup Sweet Suet Pastry.
+ Make holes in the lemon, so that it can seep.
+ Layer the raisins, butter and brown sugar one-third of the way up the bowl, put the lemon in the middle and continue layering the remaining ingredients.
+ Seal with the remainder of the pastry.
+ Put a buttered wax paper disc over the top, followed by pleated foil, and tie it with string tightly around the edges.
+ Steam for 1 1/2–2 hours, or until a knife inserted into the center comes out clean.

◆ How to Steam ◆

- ◆ With some puddings, like Spotted Dick, the ingredients are mixed into the dough; with others, like Sussex Pond Pudding, the dough has to be rolled and used to line the basin.
- ◆ Fit the dough into the pudding basin, cover loosely with pleated aluminum foil and tie with string, making sure it is tight around the edges.
- ◆ Put the pudding in a saucepan large enough and deep enough to hold the basin while covered with lid.
- ◆ Pour boiling water into the saucepan until it reaches halfway up the pudding basin. Turn the heat to medium and put the lid on top of the saucepan.
- ◆ At regular intervals, you must top up the boiling water to maintain the water level; otherwise the pudding will boil dry. Steam for 1 1/2 to 3 hours, depending on the recipe.

Spotted Dick

Oh, the hilarity and amusement of Americans when they read the menu, do a double take, then order it because they have to know what it's like to eat a spotted dick at Tea & Sympathy. It is named for the raisins in it and is also known as Spotted Dog.

SERVES 4–6
PREPARATION TIME: 3–3 1/2 hours

1 1/4 cups plump juicy raisins, white,
    brown, or a mixture
Grated rind of 1 lemon
Sweet Suet Pastry (page 109)

◆ Add the raisins and lemon rind to the pastry recipe, form the dough into a ball, and follow the steaming instructions on page 112.

OTHER IDEAS
Treacle Pudding (see page 42)

RASPBERRY JAM PUDDING
◆ Fill the bottom of the basin with jam or golden syrup until it reaches one-third of the way from the bottom and lay the unrolled pastry on top.
◆ Steam for 1 1/2–2 hours, or until a knife inserted in the center comes out clean.

CHAPTER SEVEN

Drama Queens

L ater!" Nicky calls out. "I'm popping home for a few minutes."

I can barely hear her. I've got a bad cold that crept into my ears during the night. When she reaches the door she turns around.

"I reckon that's the first time I've seen any of you clean the menus!"

I'm standing by the podium with a cloth wiping the menus, or at least that's what it looks like. I'm really learning lines. The script for my first New York play is hidden between the menus.

A few weeks ago I auditioned for a play a friend of mine had written. At the audition the director asked me to improvise a demented woman—I had just come off a shift so I was halfway there. I rolled around the floor jabbering like a monkey and for the finale I bit the director on the ankle. He was impressed. They cast me as a woman who is leaving her long-time boyfriend for a useless younger guy. She decides to leave him her foot as a memento. The new boyfriend isn't too happy about this and a conflict erupts over who gets to keep the foot.

♦ *115* ♦

The next day I tell Nicky I have a part. She is really enthusiastic and proud. "I've always believed in you," she tells me. At the staff meeting (we have only ever had three) she makes a big thing about everyone supporting me and covering my shifts.

"As soon as you know the dates," she says, "I'll get a bunch of agents to come. This is a very important opportunity."

The following day I'm making a cup of tea when I hear Lindsay say: "This Footsie is Mine?" I look up and see her reading the front of a manila envelope.

"That's for Anita," Carole says. "Some weirdo brought it in."

"It's my script," I say and snatch it out of Lindsay's hand.

"This Footsie is Mine?" She turns around; her shoulders are moving up and down.

Carole starts to laugh. "That's heading for Broadway with a name like that."

"It's a love story," I say defensively.

"What, between two feet?" says Carole.

The next thing I know Nicky's talking about getting a big group of staff and customers to come for opening night. She tells everyone I need moral support. I start to panic. The play's so bloody weird and I'm sure I'm going to be crap. In my mind I see the audience packed with regular customers: For forty-five minutes they'll watch me hop around the stage, corpsing on one foot; they'll be so embarrassed that they'll stop coming to the restaurant; worst of all, my acting dreams will be shattered. After a few sleepless nights I decide to pretend the play's been cancelled.

Nicky is mortified. "Oh Anita," she says. "You must be so disappointed."

Her reaction fills me with self-pity and my eyes well up with tears.

"Listen," she says, taking me by the shoulders and looking intensely into my eyes.

"Everything happens for a reason. Your time will come."

Carole and Lindsay were equally disappointed. They'd anticipated a good laugh at my expense.

This is how I come to be learning my lines on the sly. To make things worse, the play is opening in a week, and because of my cold my hearing is going. Tea & Sympathy's very own anonymous phone caller—a heavy-breather who is infatuated with all us waitresses—has just called and I had to tell him to speak up.

Lindsay is bent over the sideboard with her back to the restaurant while she interrogates the crank caller about his underwear. He's been calling for several months and during one conversation he said he weighed over three hundred pounds. This turned Lindsay on, so now every time he calls she hogs the telephone.

Nicky, left, with Joanna Lumley—AKA Patsy from Absolutely Fabulous, the hit British TV comedy—proudly displaying the Tea & Sympathy business card.

I'm irritated though. I don't have time to serve customers because I need to learn my lines. My character is still a mystery to me—when I asked the director for some advice, he replied, "Play it like a pimple inside-out."

♦ ♦ ♦

I repeat my lines as I go back and forth between tables. "Is that why you think I chopped it off? To be kept in a box like a prisoner?" I can hear my voice tinny and distant.

I stand beside a woman looking at her menu. Her lips are moving, but I can't hear anything: I'm now completely deaf. She closes the

Ainsley Harriott, British TV personality and chef, always comes in to eat when he is in New York.

The indelibly charming Rupert Everett in a shoot for a Japanese magazine. Rupert styled the props, insisting on using his favorite china.

menu, looks up at me, and smiles. Then her companion's lips start moving—this one's making eye contact as she orders. She stops and looks at me expectantly. She's asked a question.

"One moment please." I dash off to get Lindsay.

"My hearing's gone. Please could you take table three's order?"

Lindsay says good-bye to the caller and goes to take the order. She says something to the women, who look over sympathetically.

I was worried now. What if my hearing didn't return by opening night? How would I know when to say my lines? Could they write my deafness into the script? I stay at the back doing the drinks and feeling isolated. Lindsay comes over and says something shaking her head.

"What?" I say, twice.

Rosie with supermodel Naomi Campbell, for a story about Rosie in British Elle *magazine.*

She writes on a piece of paper: "Everyone wants fish tonight."

"Oh, right," I say in my tinny voice.

A few moments later she's back. This time she's bright red. Her hand is clapped over her mouth. She makes the number two with her finger. I look at table two and recognize a gay couple who are both regulars. I nod, showing that I understand that Lindsay doesn't want to serve them. She can't face them since she asked one of them, who's a porn star, if she could watch him making love.

"I'll wear a sheet over my head with two slits for my eyes. You'll never know I'm there." Porn star or not, the man was horrified.

"I'm sorry," I say to the two guys at table two, "but I've lost my hearing. Please could you point to what you want on the menu?"

The porn star points to the Tweed Kettle Pie and taps his wrist twice.

"You're having fish as well. Everyone's ordering fish tonight." I'm writing down their order, when suddenly they both get up and bolt out of the restaurant. The porn star touches my arm as he passes me.

I turn around to look at Lindsay. She gives me a wide-eyed look and races out as well. I'm completely bewildered. All I said was everyone's ordering fish tonight? Was there some hidden insult in those words? Why did Lindsay follow them? Maybe they saw she was working and left? And Lindsay had run after them to apologize.

My God, what a lot of drama.

The Lady Bunny in all her glory.

All this running out has agitated the remaining customers. I can't hear but I am more aware of people's body language and everyone seems very twitchy. One of the two women is waving for the check. The other one keeps staring out of the window as if she can't wait to leave.

"Please come again," I say with a smile. It's better to act as if nothing is going on. I see Nicky standing outside so I go up to the window and wave but she just glowers at me. What have I done wrong? What happened to the brownie points I'd got from cleaning the menus? I feel a bit insecure so I go and stick my head out the door. Lindsay and Nicky are standing together. Nicky's throwing up her arms like she does when she's furious.

"Come and have a cup of tea," I shout out cheerfully. Nicky stares at me. She looks really pissed off. Her shoulders drop and she shakes her head. She says something but I can't hear. I pretend not to be fazed.

"Can't chat," I say. "Got customers waiting."

As I walk back through the door it hits me. They've found out about the play!

Oh God! Well it was too late now. I'd just have to tell her the truth: that I am a big phoney, too scared to be seen on stage. I'm clearing the menus off table two when I notice they've both left their jackets. I look up and notice that the whole of the front window on the left-hand side is smashed. The door opens and Nicky and Lindsay barge in.

"Nicky!" I cry. "Someone's broken our window!"

They look at each other and collapse laughing.

◆ ◆ ◆

The next day my hearing returns and I find out what happened: While I was merrily going about my job, an irate limousine driver trying to park repeatedly reversed into the porn star's car. The star and his lover ran out and told the guy to take it easy. The driver, who was drunk, got out of the limo and shattered our window with his bare fist. Nicky came in time to see it all. She stood on the street screaming for someone to call the police. The driver and porn star had a fight. Then the NYPD came and took the limo driver away. Needless to say, Nicky had found my cheery waves somewhat puzzling.

Sandra Bernhard, actress/comedienne and one of our all-time favorite regular customers.

Postscript: "This Footsie Is Mine" was performed off-off-off-Broadway. A man from Manhattan's Public Theatre said it was easily the worst play he'd ever seen. I thought I played a pretty good pimple inside out, but it was the first and last New York play I performed in. Thank God I hadn't given up the day job.

Tweed Kettle Pie

I have to admit that I named this pie after a particularly good one I had in England many years ago. This recipe is my own version and is a good basic fish pie. We serve it with peas.

SERVES 6–8

PREPARATION TIME: 1 hour

1 lb. fresh salmon, skinned, boned and filleted
1 lb. fresh cod, skinned, boned and filleted
1 large onion, chopped
3 1/2 cups whole milk
2 bay leaves
1/4 cup (1/2 stick) butter
1/2 cup flour
1/4 cup heavy cream
2 tablespoons chopped parsley
Salt and pepper
Mashed Potato (page 93)
Grated cheese (optional)

- Preheat the oven to 350°F.
- Cut both fish into small pieces and place in a large saucepan. Add the onions, milk and bay leaves; simmer over low heat for 10–15 minutes, until the fish is cooked.
- Strain the mixture, reserve the liquid and discard the bay leaf.
- Heat the butter in a saucepan and gradually add the flour, stirring constantly until it becomes a thick paste, 2–3 minutes.
- Slowly add the milk stock, stirring constantly, then the heavy cream. Bring to a boil, then reduce the heat.
- Add the chopped parsley and remove the pan from the heat.

- Add the fish and salt and pepper to taste. Pour the mixture into a 10- to 12-inch pie dish and top with the mashed potato. Sprinkle with grated cheese, if you like.
- Bake for about 30 minutes, until golden brown.

Fish Cakes with Parsley Sauce

SERVES 8–10

PREPARATION TIME: 1 hour

1 lb. cod, boned, skinned and filleted
1 lb. salmon, boned, skinned and filleted
2 3/4 cups whole milk
2 bay leaves
1 sprig parsley
1/2 large onion, chopped
1 lb. Mashed Potato, not too soft (see page 93)
Salt and pepper
Juice of 1 lemon
1/2 cup flour
2 eggs, lightly beaten
About 1 cup fresh bread crumbs
1/2 cup oil
Parsley Sauce (see below)

- Put the fish in a pan and cover with milk. Add the bay leaves, parsley sprig, onion and a little salt and black pepper. Simmer for about 10 minutes, or until cooked.
- Remove the fish from the pan and let cool. Discard the bay leaves, onion, and parsley sprig, but reserve the liquid for the parsley sauce.

- When the fish is cool enough to handle, flake it into the mashed potatoes and season with salt and pepper and the lemon juice.
- Make patties of any size your prefer with the mixture: Roll the patties first in the flour, then in the beaten egg, and then in the bread crumbs.
- In a deep frying pan, heat the oil until it is very hot. In batches, place the fish cakes into the oil and fry until crispy and brown on both sides. As they are done, transfer them to paper towels to drain.
- Serve with Parsley Sauce (below).

PARSLEY SAUCE

1/4 cup (1/2 stick) butter
1/2 cup all-purpose flour
Stock left over from fish cakes
2 tablespoons chopped parsley
1 cup heavy cream
Salt and pepper

- Melt the butter in a frying pan. Do not let it brown.
- Add the flour, little by little, stirring with a wooden spoon, and let the roux cook for about 2 minutes.
- Gradually stir in the milky fish stock, little by little, stirring constantly until the mixture is the consistency you like.
- Add the parsley and the heavy cream; season if necessary.

OTHER IDEAS

To make parsley sauce for other dishes, you can use plain milk instead of the milky fish stock.

Faggots

Actually, faggots are really made with pig's caul, which is a little like sweetbreads. We love to call them faggots for obvious reasons, shock horror value being one of them. These are really just meatballs. Here I have made my mum's recipe, which uses the much more appetizing mixture of ground beef and pork.

SERVES 4–6

PREPARATION TIME: 1 1/2 hours

1 cup chopped onion
2 tablespoons vegetable oil
3 tablespoons butter
1/2 lb. ground beef
1/2 lb. ground pork
1 egg, beaten
1/2 teaspoon English mustard powder
2 tablespoons chopped fresh parsley
Salt and pepper
3 tablespoons flour
2 cups beef stock

+ Preheat the oven to 300°F.
+ Sauté the onion in the oil and butter until it starts to brown.
+ In a large bowl, mix the cooked onion with the beef, pork, egg, mustard, and parsley. Salt and pepper to taste. Shape the mixture into balls that fit into the palm of your hand.
+ Fry the meatballs in the remaining hot fat or vegetable oil until they are brown all over, about 10 minutes.
+ As they are done, transfer the meatballs to an ovenproof dish. After all the meat-

balls are browned, little by little stir the flour into the fat remaining in the pan until smooth.

♦ Whisk in little by little the stock and simmer for 3 minutes. Season with salt and pepper.

♦ Pour the gravy on top of the meatballs, cover with aluminum foil and bake for 45 minutes to 1 hour.

♦ Serve with mashed potatoes, Brussels sprouts, or peas.

Sticky Toffee Pudding

This pudding is much less sugary and sweet than it sounds. The real sweetness comes from the warm toffee sauce that is poured on top just before you serve it. The cake itself is not heavy and the dates give it a rich fruity flavor. It is best served warm with a dollop of whipped cream or warm custard (see page 94).

SERVES 6–8
PREPARATION TIME: 1 hour and 15 minutes

1 cup chopped dates
1 1/4 cups water
2 teaspoons pure vanilla extract
2 teaspoons strong brewed espresso coffee
1 teaspoon baking soda
3/4 cup (1 1/2 sticks) butter
3/4 cup sugar
3 eggs
1 1/2 cups all-purpose flour, sifted
1/2 teaspoon baking powder
Toffee Sauce (see below)

- Preheat the oven to 350°F.
- Simmer the dates in the water for 10 minutes, or until the dates are tender. Add the vanilla and espresso and then the baking soda; let cool.
- Cream the butter and sugar until light and fluffy, then add the eggs, one at a time. Sift in the flour and baking powder. Add the cold date mixture and mix well.
- Turn the batter into a 10-inch buttered Bundt pan and bake for 35–40 minutes, or until a knife or skewer inserted in the center comes out clean.
- Place a plate upside down over the Bundt pan and turn out the pudding onto the plate.

TOFFEE SAUCE

2 cups heavy cream
1/4 cup Tate & Lyle golden syrup
1 cup dark brown sugar

- Combine all the ingredients in a pan and boil gently for 10 minutes.
- Spoon over the pudding before serving.

CHAPTER EIGHT

Little Jimmy

I arrive for my shift feeling pretty pleased with myself. Finally I've gone to the gym and started a new regime of exercise: no more coming into work and having a whacking great piece of banana cake (my latest favorite), no more sitting down to a three-course meal. From now on it's a bowl of healthy soup and a seven-grain roll. Tonight I'm working with Rachael. She's nineteen years old and strikingly beautiful, with long black hair and amazing dark blue eyes. Her eyebrows each form a clean black arch—apparently she was born with them and they don't even need plucking? One of the advantages of working with Rachael is that you make great tips. She has no end of admirers coming in to look at her longingly. Fortunately it takes a while for them to pluck up the courage to ask her on a date. I say fortunately because she's already dating an American guy and the longer they're unaware of this, the longer I profit from the huge tips they leave. When I know Rachael better, I'll suggest she keep the boyfriend a secret. I have a hunger pang. Why not start my diet tomorrow? Rachael squeezes past to get a bread basket. I, too, look longingly

Little Jimmy, or as we like to call him (because of his demeanor and stature), Sweet 'n Low.

at her slim-fit jeans and nineteen-year-old bottom. Piously I put my order in for a bowl of watercress soup.

Little Jimmy is working in the kitchen. He's about five feet two, but the kitchen floor is elevated, so he looks tall.

"Thanks, Little Jimmy," I say, putting the check on the hatch.

He picks up the check and tosses it behind him.

"Jimmy!"

"Filthy ass," he says.

"I beg your pardon?"

He ignores me and throws a handful of mixed greens into a stainless-steel bowl. He pours in salad dressing from a plastic container and mixes the salad with metal tongs. He says something in Spanish. Pancho, who must be standing by the sink out of view, laughs.

"Jimmy? What's wrong with you?"

Little Jimmy continues to ignore me. I catch the expression in his eyes and I know he's not joking. I've known him long enough to see when he's angry. I have no idea why though. Only yesterday I'd stood by the kitchen laughing with him. What on earth had happened since?

I step out of view of the hatch and ask Rachael.

"Is Little Jimmy funny with you?"

"Funny?" says Rachael shrugging her shoulders. "No, he's normal. Why?"

I tell her what he did. Rachael walks to the hatch and says in her Liverpudlian accent, "Little Jimmy, why won't you give Anita a bowl of watercress soup?"

"It is not your business, my darling."

"Yes, it is, because she's my friend."

I pull Rachael away and tell her not to bother. I hope that whatever's wrong will be sorted out before the night's over.

Later on, Pancho comes to empty the bus trays.

"Pancho. What's up with Little Jimmy?"

Pancho's round, friendly face closes up. That's the trouble: There's this kitchen solidarity, which isn't helped by the fact none of us speaks Spanish. They, however, have the uncanny ability to overhear us and understand every nuance of our chat.

I grab Pancho's arm. "I'm not letting you back in the kitchen until you tell me."

He looks away. "Little Jimmy very angry with you."

"I can see that. Why?"

"You no remember yesterday?"

"Yesterday? What about yesterday?"

Pancho looks at me as if I'm lying.

"Yes, you remember. You slap his face."

"Slap his face?" And then I remembered. "Oh yes! But he kept grabbing my arse. It was a friendly slap!"

"Still, Anita, it's no good you slap his face. He very shame. Customers see you. Jimmy very angry."

"But that's ridiculous. It wasn't a hard slap. Besides what's worse—customers seeing me slap his face, or seeing the chef grab my arse?"

Pancho shakes his head as if I've missed the point. "I don't know. He no want to talk to you."

I know there's no way that I'm going to make Pancho see it from my point of view. It's that whole macho thing. You never know when you've stepped over this invisible line of pride, but when you do they certainly make you pay for it.

As I take orders, I try to ignore the un-

Rachael at the hot-water nozzle. Oh, how we miss her!

pleasant sensation in the pit of my stomach. It's such a small restaurant that harmony among the staff is crucial. There's nowhere to hide—you have to interact with each other whether you like it or not.

I ask Clezio for *trapos*. He sneaks a sidelong look at Little Jimmy before he puts a pile of them on the hatch. When Little Jimmy is in the toilet, I ask Pancho to make me a sandwich. I'm getting hungry. Pancho avoids eye contact and sort of nods, but the sandwich never arrives.

About nine o'clock, Rachael orders herself a vegetable cottage pie. The plan is to put her name on the check and then give it to me.

Little Jimmy studies the check. "I'm not going to make this for you Rachael. You know I love you, my darling, but I think you gonna give this to filthy ass."

"For Christ's sake, Jimmy. Don't be so bloody ridiculous!" I scream.

Little Jimmy responds in a low, growling litany of what must be Spanish insults. The last one is *puta*. There are gales of laughter from Pancho and Clezio. I hate them all.

Louise, another one of our favorite girls.
This picture was taken at Christmastime.

The next night Little Jimmy is off. Clezio and Noel, the two Brazilians, are working and the night passes smoothly.

The following morning, I walk through the door and see Little Jimmy. He looks up, grimaces, and says something in Spanish. I decide I'm going to ignore him, but if he calls me a *puta*, I'm marching into that kitchen and smacking him around the head with a pan.

Around one o'clock I write my name on a check and put in an order for a bowl of lentil soup. Jimmy just tosses the check over his shoulder. I go and seat two customers who have just walked in. It feels as if my heart is in my throat. Next I take table three's order, the man wants mustard in his ham sandwich. I tell Jimmy this as I pass him the check. He looks up and stares through me as if I'm invisible. He does put the mustard in the sandwich though.

Later I watch Lindsay standing in the kitchen telling him about her collection of porn videos. Little Jimmy touches her thigh with his hand. "I think we should make a video. First we must go to the basement to practice."

At three o'clock Little Jimmy walks out of the restaurant wearing a T-shirt and jeans. "Good-bye, my darling," he says to Lindsay. She bends down and kisses his cheek. He doesn't even look in my direction.

Later when I go to the bathroom I see that somebody has torn a photograph of me in half. That's it, I decide. I'm leaving. I'm in an impossible situation. I can't say anything to Nicky because that would be snitching, and if

An interior photo of Tea & Sympathy, *which was first published in* Old Greenwich Village.

you think a slap around the face is bad, snitching is unforgivable. I'd have all the kitchen staff against me. Besides Little Jimmy is an excellent cook, fast and good. Nicky won't want there to be any trouble between us. I even really like him. We all do. He's even got the nickname Sweet 'n Low. I love his dimples, his expressive brown eyes, and infectious laughter. He has a great talent for mimicry and can do fantastic impressions of all of us. But if he wasn't going to forgive me I couldn't stay. I'd have to go somewhere else.

That night when I go home, I call Carole to tell her about Little Jimmy and my decision to leave. She says she knows how I feel because when she first started working, Little Jimmy didn't speak to her for a fortnight. And she never even found out why.

"Carole I can't stand it," I moan. "I'm weak. I don't like being hated. It's too stressful."

"Before you do anything drastic," she says, "come round now. I've got a bottle of wine. Let's talk about it."

♦ ♦ ♦

A couple of years ago, Carole decided to leave Tea & Sympathy. Nicky didn't stop crying for days.

"I don't know what I'm going to do without that girl," she kept repeating. "Tea & Sympathy just won't be the same without her."

There was a farewell dinner and Nicky and Sean presented her with a specially inscribed pen, which she then lost a few days later.

If anyone mentioned Carole's name, Nicky's eyes welled up with tears and her hand instinctively went to her heart. My mistake was to report all this to Carole, because a month later she was back. It was like the return of the prodigal daughter, she got the best shifts, and I don't think I ever saw her clean the fridge again.

Later, she confessed to me that she'd missed working at the restaurant. This was my fear as well. Whenever I seriously thought of leaving I felt this huge void inside. Tea & Sympathy was more than just a job. It was my social life and my family. Once we were all sitting in Fiddlesticks when a friend of one of the waitresses who was visiting from England said something like "Doesn't it bother you just being a waitress?" I remember being really surprised. I'd never really thought about the status aspect before. In many ways that is one reason why America is so popular among the Brits: That whole class thing is absent; Americans seem more interested in where you are now than where you went to school. And in an odd way (not that we ever really thought about it like this), Tea & Sympathy had become a trendy place to work; it had a certain cachet.

For me, its intimacy and eccentricity put me in touch with people from all walks of life. Why just the day before I'd had a chat with two cops from our local precinct: One of them showed me a hole in his pants that he'd got from chasing a burglar to the West Side Highway and then bending underneath a car to arrest him. Then I'd watched Harold Evans, former editor of *The Times* of London and leader of the New York Brit Pack, clean the gutter outside Tea & Sympathy (he'd insisted that Nicky should not have to do it herself). Not to mention an X-rated story Bob next door told me about a delivery he'd just made (who cared whether or not it really happened?).

In all my years of waitressing at Tea & Sympathy I've never been bored. People are rarely boring, and especially not for the duration of a meal or a cup of tea. On my way to Carole's, I reflected with much regret on my decision to leave.

A couple of bottles of wine later, I'd forgotten most of my worries, although I'd not yet worked out what to do. Then, as I was about to leave, Carole told me what I had to do to get round Little Jimmy: flirt.

"You know what," she slurred. "Tomorrow when I go in, I'll tell him that you're really upset. I'll say to him, 'You know Anita's been in love with you for years?' That ought to do it."

"Great idea," I said and stumbled off home.

When I go to work the next night, Little Jimmy looks up. He looks quickly down again but at least he doesn't pull a face. To help the flirting along I'm wearing black tights and a short skirt. Nice and easy if he fancies a swipe at my *bunda*.

"Hi," I say to him and Noel.

"Anita, you sexy," says Noel, the shy Brazilian chef with the sweet smile. Little Jimmy ignores me, but there's no disparaging aside in Spanish. This is an improvement.

I take table three's order. They want two tuna fish sandwiches. I put the check on the hatch. Little Jimmy picks up the check.

"They want white bread or seven grain?"

"Hang on, Jimmy. I'll just ask them." I come back. "Both on seven grain."

"Okay," he says.

My spirits soar. Carole is taking table eight's order. She looks over at me and I give her the thumbs-up.

I go to the toilet a couple of times but Little Jimmy still hasn't softened enough to grab me. On the third time, he follows me into the toilet and puts his hands around my waist.

"Let me see your hairy ass?"

"Jimmy!"

"I know the English girls have a hairy ass."

Sweet 'n Low, right, with his brother George— sweet, but not so low.

"How do you know?" I look down at him with a dirty smile.

"Because, my darling, this is my job to know."

Postscript: Luckily, I was saved by the kitchen bell, although Jimmy did give my arse a further squeeze before returning to the kitchen. Carole was right, however: Flirting really works. I'd seriously recommend it to any young waitress having trouble with a chef.

Vegetable Stock

Yₒu can always opt for using store-bought bouillon cubes in any flavor or canned stock, but it does taste better and less salty if you use fresh homemade stock, especially for soup. If you want a good chicken stock then just add a whole chicken to this recipe. For a good beef stock, just add chopped up meat bones, roasted until they are brown. You can usually get these from your local butcher.

MAKES APPROXIMATELY 15 CUPS

5 carrots, peeled and chopped
5 stalks celery, chopped
3 leeks, washed and trimmed
2 onions, peeled and quartered
2 parsnips, peeled and chopped
2 cloves garlic, peeled and halved
A few sprigs parsley
2 bay leaves
2 tablespoons chopped mixed herbs,
    fresh or dry
Salt and pepper to taste
15 cups water

- Combine all the ingredients in a large saucepan and bring to a boil, then reduce the heat to very low and simmer gently for 3–4 hours.
- Strain the stock; discard the solids.

Parsnip Soup

*P*arsnips are not used in America very often even though they are readily available. I love the sweetness that they add to any kind of stew or soup. At the restaurant, we always make soup vegetarian and dairy free, but you may use chicken stock if you wish. I prefer mine with the chicken stock and then blended with a swirl of heavy cream in the middle. Serve this soup with fresh crunchy rolls and butter.

SERVES 6–8

PREPARATION TIME: 1 hour and 15 minutes

1/4 cup (1/2 stick) butter
1 large onion, chopped
2 stalks celery, washed and chopped
1 large potato, peeled and chopped
6 large parsnips, peeled and chopped
6 cups vegetable or chicken stock
3 bay leaves
Salt & pepper
2–4 tablespoons milk or cream (optional)

- Melt the butter in a large saucepan and sauté the onion and celery until they are soft.
- Add the potato, parsnips, stock and bay leaves and simmer for 40 minutes, or until the vegetables are soft.
- Season with salt and pepper and, if you like, add a swirl of milk or cream.
- You can puree the soup in a blender and serve with a swirl of cream or leave it chunky.

Watercress Soup

Watercress is normally used in salad or as a garnish for meat and fish dishes. This soup is pale in color and delicate in flavour and is an ideal summer soup. It can be served hot or chilled. Either way garnish it with a little fresh watercress.

SERVES 6–8

PREPARATION TIME: 1 hour and 15 minutes

1/4 cup (1/2 stick) butter
1 onion, peeled and chopped
2 large leeks (white part only), washed thoroughly and chopped
2 medium potatoes, washed, peeled and chopped
Salt and pepper
7 1/2 cups chicken or vegetable stock
2 bunches watercress, washed, trimmed and roughly chopped
1/2 cup plus 2 tablespoons heavy cream (optional)

- Melt the butter in a large saucepan and cook the onion and leeks until soft.
- Add the potatoes and salt and pepper to taste. Cover the pan and sweat the vegetables over low heat, stirring occasionally, for about 15 minutes.
- Add the stock and watercress and bring to a simmer. Cover and cook for 10–15 minutes.
- Remove the pan from the heat and remove the lid; allow to cool.
- When the soup has cooled, puree it gently in a blender.
- Return the pureed soup to the pan and reheat before serving. Season as necessary.
- Stir in the cream, if using, just before serving.

Leek & Potato Soup

*T*his is another of my mother's much made and enjoyed recipes. Leeks are abundant in Welsh cookery. They must be washed thoroughly or your soup will be gritty. I rinse them first, chop, and then rinse them again. Again, this can be served chilled in the summer. You may puree this soup in a blender or leave it chunky.

SERVES 6–8

PREPARATION TIME: 45 minutes

1/4 cup (1/2 stick) butter
4 medium leeks (white part only),
  washed thoroughly and finely chopped
1 onion, peeled and chopped
3 potatoes, peeled and chopped
2 teaspoons salt
7 1/2 cups vegetable or chicken stock
Pepper
4 tablespoons cream (optional)

- Melt the butter in a large saucepan and cook the leeks and onion over medium heat until they are soft but not brown.
- Add the potatoes, salt and stock and simmer for 35–40 minutes, or until the potatoes are soft.
- When ready to serve, reheat and crack a little black pepper over the top. Swirl in some cream, if desired.

Stilton & Walnut Salad

Stilton is a rich creamy blue cheese made in England and this salad is the most popular at Tea & Sympathy. We use tart green apples, but you may use sweeter red apples or substitute ripe pear slices for the apples. If you cannot get Stilton cheese, use a good blue cheese, such as French Roquefort.

SERVES 1

PREPARATION TIME: 20 minutes

1 handful mesclun per serving
Balsamic Vinaigrette (see page 140)
4 tablespoons crumbled Stilton cheese
1/2 apple, chopped into bite-size pieces
3 tablespoons walnut halves

- Toss the mesclun with the dressing.
- Arrange the cheese, apples, and walnuts atop the greens.

Beet Salad

*K*nown as beetroot in England, beets are another vegetable that you do not see a lot on restaurant menus in New York. Do not overcook them because they lose their flavor and rich purple-red color. Once the beets have been tossed in the vinaigrette they may be added to any kind of greens. They are also fantastic added to the Stilton & Walnut salad (see page 138). At Tea & Sympathy, this is known as Sean Salad, because my husband came up with the idea of adding them to the Stilton Salad.

SERVES 4–6

PREPARATION TIME: Approximately 1 hour

6 large or 12 medium beets, gently washed
    so as not to break the skin
1 medium onion, peeled and thinly sliced
Balsamic Vinaigrette (see page 140)
1 handful mesclun per serving

+ Put the beets into salted boiling water and cook until tender (time will vary according to size), but do not stab them to see if they are ready, or they will bleed. When you can remove the skin easily with your fingers, it usually means that the beets are cooked.
+ When the beets are ready, strain them and remove the skins. Let them cool a little, and then cut them into bite-size chunks.
+ Add the onion and the vinaigrette; toss to combine.
+ Spoon some of the beet and onion mixture over each serving of mesclun. You will not need to dress the greens as there will already be enough dressing in the beets and onions.

Balsamic Vinaigrette

This is the dressing we use on salads in the restaurant. It is a nice simple base to which you may want to add fresh herbs (chives, parsley, tarragon or basil) or a touch of raspberry jam for more flavour.

SERVES 6 AS A SALAD

6 tablespoons good-quality olive oil
1 teaspoon English mustard powder
3 tablespoons balsamic vinegar
1/2 teaspoon salt and freshly ground black pepper
1 clove garlic, crushed (optional)

♦ Combine all the ingredients in a screw-top jar and shake vigorously until everything has blended. Taste before dressing the salad. If it seems a little bland then add a little more salt.

♦ Tarragon Vinaigrette ♦

For a change from the balsamic, tarragon is always nice. The same instructions and serving suggestions apply.

1/2 cup olive oil
1/4 cup tarragon vinegar
1 rounded teaspoon Dijon mustard

1/2 teaspoon honey mustard
Salt and pepper

Potato Salad

An American staple, we serve this only in the summer with chilled poached salmon or smoked trout.

SERVES 6–8

For the salad:
3 lbs. potatoes
1 onion, finely chopped
1 tablespoon chopped parsley
4 sliced scallions or spring onions
1 tablespoon chopped chives (optional)

For the mayonnaise:
2 eggs
1/2 teaspoon Dijon mustard
1/2 tablespoon white wine vinegar
1 clove garlic, peeled and crushed
Salt and pepper
3/4 cup sunflower oil
3/4 cup olive oil

- Peel and halve the potatoes. Cook in boiling salted water for about 20 minutes, or until soft. Once cooked cool them by submerging them in cold water.
- Combine the onion, parsley and scallions in a bowl and put aside.
- To prepare the mayonnaise, combine the eggs, mustard, vinegar, garlic and salt and pepper in a food processor. With the motor running, pour the oils slowly through the feed tube. The mayonnaise will thicken.
- Add the mayonnaise to the onion, parsley and scallion mixture. Cube the cooled potatoes and add them to the herbed mayonnaise; toss to combine.
- Add salt and pepper to taste. Garnish with chopped fresh chives, if you like.

CHAPTER NINE

Changeover

As I step into the restaurant at five o'clock I give it a quick once-over. Four tables are remaining: three finishing up cream teas and the fourth, Mr. N, who's tucking into his sandwich. Good! No orders to take. Time for a cup of tea and a gossip.

The period from five to five-thirty is referred to as Changeover. This is when the night shift arrives to replace the day shift. For half an hour we are all together, theoretically creating a smooth transition from day to night.

Carole is sitting on the stool at the podium eating a Bakewell Tart. She's been working with Baby Lynsay (not to be confused with Naughty Lindsay, who's about to arrive any minute), which means she's had a nice easy shift. Baby Lynsay is our most recent arrival. She's fresh off a Sussex farm and has an English Rose complexion and beautiful clear blue eyes. Robert's afraid we're corrupting her with our fast living. He doesn't realize she can drink all of us under the table.

As I pass the counter I see Baby Lynsay on her hands and knees cleaning the fridge.

"You look busy," I say, kissing Carole on the cheek.

"She likes doing the lists," she says defensively. "Besides she's young. Give her a few years and she'll be as vile as me."

Now that I'm here Carole starts to do the bank. It's not because she has a flair for accountancy but because it gets her out of cleaning and writing the list. The list has to be done during Changeover and it's an unpopular chore. You have to get on your knees and rummage around the fridge trying to calculate how many sodas need to be ordered for the night and the following day. Also you have to check the shelves to see if we need ketchup, HP Sauce, Branston Pickle, piccalilli, Marmite, English mustard, sugar, barleywater, Ribena, coffee filters, take-out cups, and aluminum containers to pack up people's doggy bags: Americans always take their leftovers home.

The list is given to the kitchen staff. When they have time, someone goes down to the basement and brings up the orders in a crate, which you then have to unpack. When young Rachael does the list it looks like calligraphy. At the end she writes "Thank You" and draws a smiley face.

Next, the tea tins must be carried next door to our British store and replenished, then the clotted cream and jam containers filled up. This is our busiest period for the afternoon, and for cream teas.

Before, we had to write the dinner specials on the blackboard but now they're printed out and attached to the menus with a paper clip.

I make a big pot of tea and put it on table one with four mugs. Baby Lynsay's already done the cleaning, the list, and everything else.

When the restaurant is very busy Changeover can be manic. Everything feels out of control. Customers come and go without you even registering them. Carole once tried to seat people she'd spent the past hour serving. They were getting up to leave. "Table for two?" she asked them and wondered why they looked hurt.

At around five-fifteen, whoever is doing the bank might start barking orders to put checks down on tables. It gives customers fifteen minutes to finish their tea and pay. After five-thirty the tips belong to the night shift. It's a horrible feeling when the big table you've just spent the last couple of hours serving goes and orders another pot of tea just as you're about to stick the check on the table.

"Another pot of tea?" you repeat incredulously to the guilty party. Sometimes this works and they might say, "On second thought, I've had enough." But more often than not, you have to take the check back. While you make their tea you can't help calculating the amount of the lost tip.

At five-thirty, the red tea tin, which holds the tips, is emptied onto the wooden top of the podium. The mainly dollar bills, sometimes the odd fives, are counted and divided into two piles. This moment signals not just the physical split of changing shifts, but also the beginning of an emotional shift, as powerful undercurrents of jealousy and self-interest, never talked about but palpable in this tiny space, rise to the surface. Like now, as Carole and Baby Lynsay, their heads bowed as if in prayer, count the mound of bills. These are the fruits of their labor. They join them body and soul.

Lindsay and I sit on table one drinking our tea. The counting of the tips distracts us. The unity of the past half-hour, the jokes, the gossip and shared confidences, has come to an end: It's us and them. Instinctively we stop talking. We want to hear how much money they made. The figure is nearly always said aloud, in triumph or dismay. I don't hear how much they made, but they shake hands. They must have done well. Carole leans back against the wall content. She lights a cigarette and gives me a sweet smile.

"Good day?" I ask innocently.

"Brilliant," she says.

"That's great." Inside, I'm experiencing the inevitable sinking feeling. If the day shift does really well then more than likely the night will be dead. It seems to be a general rule. Conversely, if they had made crap money, I'd have made a sympathetic face—and felt a surge of hope.

This might all sound petty but it really doesn't last long. As soon as we've kissed Baby Lynsay and Carole good-bye, our shift officially begins, and with the dimming of the lights comes the promise of a busy night.

Lindsay takes a little black apron out of a drawer under the sideboard. She puts it on over her jeans and sticks a pen in the pocket. Leaning against the metal surface of the fridge, she folds her arms and stares out of the window.

Mr. N on table six lifts up his iced tea glass. This means he wants a free refill. Mr. N is a Russian millionaire with an unpronounceable last name. He has a bushy black beard and is fat and distinguished. He often parks his Porsche outside and makes a big deal about getting in and out, looking from side to side to clock who's watching. The last time he was in he spent about twenty minutes telling me that it's time I thought of marriage. I kept trying to tell him I didn't have a boyfriend, but he wouldn't stop talking to listen.

When we're not busy I often watch Mr. N eat his tuna salad sandwich. He holds half a sandwich in one hand and a handkerchief in the other. Every now and then he wipes his forehead and takes a slurp of iced tea. He gets this drowsy look when he's eating, as if the sandwich is sapping his energy. When he's finished he takes a fat finger and drags it over his plate picking up stray crumbs and dropped bits of tuna. He licks his finger, and does it again.

At five to six the restaurant door is flung open. Terry, one of our American regulars, rushes in red-faced and out of breath. "Is it still lunch?"

I look at the clock above the coffee machine. "It's five minutes to six."

"Thank God!" he says and slumps into a chair on table one.

At six o'clock dinner officially begins. There's not an awful lot of difference in the dishes except in price. At dinner everything is more expensive. I never understood why this was until Nicky pointed out that people spend much longer over dinner, so the turnover is that much slower.

In Terry's case the only thing on the lunch menu that attracts him are the prices. He's notoriously stingy. Once he arrived in about the same state as today and as a joke Carole told him that he was too late, we were already on dinner. He looked so stricken I thought he was going to have a heart attack.

"I'm kidding," Carole said quickly.

Terry gets his tea on the house because he was one of our early regulars. The tradition began with Robert, who still gets tea and dessert free. When Rachael first started working, she didn't know about Terry's free tea and added it to his bill. When he looked at the check I actually saw the blood drain from his face.

"No, no!" he told Rachael. "I don't pay for my tea. I'm in Nicky's tea club!"

I take Terry's order. He wants a side of banger, a side of mash, and a side of beans. I wonder why he's ordered each item separately and not just a plate of bangers, mash, and beans? I look at the menu and see that this way he's saved a dollar fifty. When the three side orders arrive, he asks for a bigger plate, so he can put them together. Part of me doesn't want to give him the big plate, but I do.

I like Terry. He's friendly and curious. He always asks me how I am, and listens to my answers. He's genuinely moved by others' misfortunes. He told me that he grew up in real poverty in Chicago. Once I knew that, I understood that he couldn't help himself: His fear of poverty was something visceral, his anxiety real and undisguised. I saw Terry's stinginess as a sort of sickness.

Most of our customers are very generous but over the years some strange stingy natures have been revealed. For instance we used to take a dining card and most of the customers who used it turned out to be bad tippers. Carole boasted that she could spot one of these cardholders a mile off.

"It's written all over their faces," she'd say.

No matter how well you served them they'd give you either the exact percentage of tip or much less. They'd tip cents. Things like one dollar, twenty two cents. They couldn't bring themselves to round it off to a dollar fifty, which psychologically for us is a lot less demoralizing.

There are some warning signs. For instance if you've given a table a check and they ask for two separate bills, you know the tip will be small. The same applies if they ask to borrow the calculator—a bad sign that means neither of them wants to pay a cent more than

Richard and Marisa, Brits in New York.

his fair share. When it comes to leaving a tip, the same rule applies. One time I served this really lovely group of women. They were from South Carolina and we couldn't have got on better. I let them have little tastes of the desserts and gave them loads of refills, even putting fresh tea in their pots. When they left, Rachael, who had picked up the check from the table, told me that they hadn't left a tip. I had never run after a customer before, although Carole had plenty of times. This time, however, I was really hurt. I wanted to know why. Maybe it was a mistake? I went running out the door.

"Excuse me," I called out. They stopped walking and turned around. I caught up with them.

"I'm sorry," I said. "But was there something wrong with the service?"

"Not at all," one of them said replied.

"Oh. I just wondered because you didn't leave a tip." My face was flaming.

"But I'm sure we did," they said. The one I'd really liked pulled out her purse and took out ten dollars. "Would this be enough?" She asked.

I took the money and said thank you. I walked back to the restaurant regretting it deeply. The lovely relationship I'd enjoyed with them inside the restaurant had been ruined by my greed.

"I'm sorry," Rachael said as I walked through the door. "I tried to call you back. They left a really nice tip, but it was hidden between the check."

I literally died with shame. It was the last time I made a fuss about a tip. As Nicky always says, in the end it makes no difference: The big tippers, of whom there are happily many, always make up for the small tippers.

For the next hour there are no customers. Lindsay and I stand by the podium reading

Hello magazine. I've just coloured in the queen's hair with black pen. I draw a little arrow and write the word *Carole*.

Mr. N appears by the podium. "My two favorite waitresses," he says passing Lindsay his check and money. "I'm here to beg a small favor."

"What can we do for you Mr. N?" Lindsay says in a flirty tone.

"That's the spirit," he says. "Now I'm sure I mentioned that my dear son will be arriving for a holiday from Russia. He is a mere eighteen years old."

"I didn't know you had a son that old, Mr. N?" Lindsay says.

"A young and innocent mistake when I was but a mere lad. The problem is the dear boy hasn't yet fully become a man."

Our expressions must have been blank.

"He's still a virgin." Mr. N explains. "Well it crossed my mind that one of the girls here might render a small service, and break in the young colt."

"You mean go to bed with him?" asks Lindsay.

"My dear, I didn't mention bed. However if that's what's needed to expedite the matter, then bed it is. I'll leave it in your capable hands to decide on the best course of action." Mr. N gives a little bow, and waddles out of the restaurant.

Lindsay looks at me. "Do you believe that, Nits? He expects us to shag his son?"

"Unbelievable," I say, shaking my head.

"Don't get me wrong, I've got nothing against doing an eighteen-year-old virgin, but what a bloody cheek! He's only tipped us a dollar!"

Postscript: Tight Terry discovered a less stressful way of ensuring himself lunch prices by telephoning in his order before six o'clock. He moved back to Chicago, but the last time I served him he asked if he could have a half-portion of apple crumble and custard. I said I was sorry but it wasn't possible. "Okay," he said. "Give me one spoonful less and knock off a dollar."

Mr. N did bring in his virgin son, but alas it was on Lindsay's day off and the young colt had to go elsewhere to be broken in.

Egg & Bacon Tart

*T*his is another childhood passion. When my mum comes to visit I insist on her making this. It is her recipe and it is the mashed potato base that makes it different from the traditional version. If you are a vegetarian, you may omit the bacon and add a little more onion or lightly steamed small florets of broccoli. Serve with a mixed green salad. This is a typical dish that would be served for high tea, which is not to be confused with afternoon tea.

SERVES 8–10

PREPARATION TIME: 1 1/2 hours

Savoury Pastry (see page 110)
1 cup Mashed Potato (see page 93)
5 eggs
1/2 cup heavy cream
1/2 cup grated sharp Cheddar cheese
Salt and pepper
2 tablespoons butter
2 cups diced bacon
1 1/2 cups onion, peeled and thinly sliced

- Preheat the oven to 375°F.
- Place a baking tray large enough to hold a 10-inch pie dish in the oven. Line the pie dish with savoury pastry and then a thin layer of mashed potato about 1/4 inch thick.
- In a bowl beat the eggs. Add the cream, grated Cheddar cheese and salt and pepper to taste.
- Melt the butter in a pan. Add the bacon and the onions and cook until soft. When the onions start to brown, remove the pan from the heat.

- Turn the contents of the pan onto the mashed potato and then cover with the egg mixture.
- Place the tart on the baking tray. This helps to ensure that the pastry cooks all the way through. Bake 30–40 minutes.

Bakewell Tart

This tart is thought to have originated at the Rutland Arms in Bakewell, England. The legend goes that an inexperienced cook accidentally omitted the flour in an almond sponge. It should be served at room temperature and does not need any sauce or custard. They may be made as small tarts, but remember the baking time will be a little less.

SERVES 10–12

PREPARATION TIME: 1 hour and 15 minutes

1/2 lb. Sweet Pastry (see page 107)
2 tablespoons raspberry jam
2 eggs, beaten
1/2 cup sugar
1/2 cup melted butter
1 cup ground almonds
1 tablespoon flour
A few drops of almond extract
1 cup confectioners' sugar
About 2 tablespoons water
Glacé cherries (optional)

- Preheat the oven to 350°F.
- Place a baking tray large enough to hold a 9-inch pie dish in the oven.
- Line the pie dish with the sweet pastry and spread the jam evenly over the bottom of the pastry.
- Beat the butter and sugar in a large bowl until thick and pale. Add the eggs a little at a time, then add the almond extract. Fold in the flour and ground almonds and mix thoroughly.
- Pour the mixture into the pastry and bake for 40 minutes or until the filling is just set and browned.
- Place the tart on the baking sheet while it is cooking.
- When the tart is cool, mix the confectioners' sugar with the water, pour over the top of the cake, and let set. Garnish with glacé cherries, if you like.

Lemon Curd

Delicious rich lemon curd may be spread on scones or toast, English muffins or sponge cake. You may substitute lime for some or all of the lemon for a sharper flavor.

MAKES 2 CUPS
PREPARATION TIME: 45 minutes

1/4 cup (1/2 stick) butter, melted
4 eggs
1 cup sugar
Juice and rind of 3 small or 2 large lemons

- Melt the butter, then beat in the eggs.
- Stir in the sugar and beat until thoroughly combined.
- Gradually add the lemon rind and juice.

♦ Cook in a double boiler over simmering water, stirring constantly, until the mixture thickens.

♦ Remove from the heat and let cool. Make sure the lemon curd is thoroughly cooled before using it.

Note: If you do not have a double boiler you can use a stainless steel bowl set over a regular saucepan of gently boiling water.

CHAPTER TEN

Claudia

I t's a slow Monday night. Only a few regulars are dotted about the tables and outside it's cold and dark. It's meant to snow later.

"Carole," I say. "How about playing the Claudia game?"

Carole shakes her head. "No."

"Oh, go on. It's fun!"

"No, it bloody isn't. Last time I felt depressed for days." The way she says it, though, I know she won't take much persuading.

Claudia was a Tea & Sympathy regular. She kept us all amused, including the kitchen boys. As soon as she walked through the door she'd make for the kitchen hatch, point her finger at the cooks and say, "You're fired!" They were always taken aback, mainly because for most of the customers they remained invisible.

Claudia first started coming when she was spending a lot of time visiting a friend of hers with AIDS at St. Vincent's Hospital. She'd visit him and then stop in at the restaurant for a cup of tea and a portion of sympathy before going on to a much-hated waitressing post.

Over the years she entertained Carole and me with many stories about the succession of strange, or just mundane, jobs that supported her while she auditioned. It always seemed like she was either just beginning a job or had just left one. If it wasn't busy, we sat on table one, drinking tea and eating cake while we chatted about men and diets. She was warm, funny, and vulnerable, with a Brooklyn accent that I loved to imitate.

One night Claudia came in and said that a friend had suggested she write something. It was pretty clear to Claudia that it should be about her life and struggles in New York. We didn't see her for a long time and then I went away to England on holiday. I called Nicky to tell her when I'd be back.

"Well you know who's become an overnight success?" she asked. "Claudia Shear. Do you remember her?"

Libby and Amanda or Amanda and Libby, the breakfast twins! They once did a runner, but we found them laughing in the store next door!

I came back to New York and it was true: Claudia had become a star. Her play, "Blown Sideways Through Life," had moved from the New York Theater Workshop to off-Broadway at the Cherry Lane Theatre. It told the story of the sixty-four temporary jobs she'd held, from whorehouse receptionist to Wall Street proofreader. *The New York Times* had called it "a touching striptease of the soul." Nicky had even been to the previews.

"You should have seen her," she said. "She got a standing ovation. People were literally blown away. I couldn't stop crying."

Of course Claudia's "overnight" success wasn't really a question of luck; she'd made it happen. But she was the first person I knew who had been a waitress, like me, and was now writing scripts for Hollywood.

Every now and then Nicky would call from next door, "Save table one. Claudia's coming." And my heart would sink. Not because I didn't still like her— I did—but because her fame had become an issue for me. Now customers recognized her, and I no longer knew how to relate to her. She still came in to chat and tell her stories, but what had changed was the way I listened. Whereas before I might be stacking teapots or adding up a check, half-listening to her voice as it cut into the Tom Jones CD, sometimes laughing, sometimes ignoring her, now I felt I had to give her all my attention. It was a weird dilemma: I worried that if

I paid her too much attention, she'd think I was sucking up, but then if I didn't pay her enough attention she might think I was jealous (which, I suppose, I was). I couldn't be natural.

One night I was sitting on table one feeling depressed about my life, mainly because of an unfaithful boyfriend, when I heard the familiar words "You're fired!"

Claudia sat down next to me and then Carole joined us, quickly telling Claudia that I was depressed. I was so down that I forgot my inhibitions concerning Claudia. Before I knew it, we were drinking tea and chatting about relationships. It was just like the old days. Claudia was the exact same person, except that now she was famous. I was coming to understand that the most final thing about success was the way other people perceived you.

Once, sitting in the restaurant at the same time, but on different tables, were Judi Dench, Rupert Everett and Quentin Tarantino. Nicky walked in, took one look at them and said, "Blimey look at you lot! Three of you all in here together." They all sort of tuttered, embarrassed, but Nicky was just expressing what we all thought. An invisible thread of fame linked up the tables like a constellation, a thread that no one could ignore even though we all pretended to. Now Claudia had crossed into this sphere too, and so her experience became the premise of "the Claudia game" that Carole and I would play on a quiet night. Of course, Claudia never behaved as I did playing the game.

"Come on, Carole. It's dead tonight," I say. "We're going to make bugger all money. Let's play Claudia and at least have some fun."

"But it's not fun," said Carole childishly, her bottom lip sticking out.

She was already getting a bit into character so I persisted. "Please!"

"All right then," she says finally. "But only on the condition I get to be the successful one after you."

"Okay," I say. I gather up my bags, put on a coat and leave the restaurant. I stand outside in the cold. I look through the window. It is bright and cheerful inside. There are only three customers. Chicken & Leek Pie sits on table nine reading a big book, probably nonfiction, something to do with computers or science. He comes in every night and all he ever wants is a chicken and leek pie, a glass of water, and an ashtray. He doesn't care about small talk, plus he leaves a nice tip—a perfect customer.

Sourpuss and her husband sit on table six. The husband now wants us to serve his ginger beer to him in the can. He's found out that when we pour it into a glass, a centimeter of soda remains in the can and gets chucked out. They both love Carole, which is good because I don't have to bother with them. I wait until Carole has served them their two tweed kettle pies before I make my entrance.

When I play Claudia I completely zone out the restaurant. I'm not even aware if any of the customers are watching. I'm too focused on Carole. She looks up feigning total surprise. "Anita!" she says.

"Oh my God, Carole! Don't tell me you are still here?"

Carole nods sheepishly. "You look beautiful!"

I give her a hug. "Thank you. I'm actually exhausted. I've just been filming, and it's a crazy schedule. How's Nicky? I can't wait to see her."

"Nicky's fine," Carole says. She takes a *trapo* and begins cleaning the sideboard. "You're making a film? That must be exciting."

"Right now it's just absolutely exhausting." (I change my voice for this role: it's deep and authoritative.) "We finished today. Now the partying starts. There's a big do at Uma and Ethan's. Johnny Depp's coming."

"Really?" Carole looks up wistfully. "I . . . I don't suppose I could come?"

"I'd love you to . . . but it's sort of invitation only."

"Oh, right." Carole takes a tub of cutlery from the hatch. She organizes it into the plastic trays.

"Nothing's changed." I look around. " I can't believe I ever worked here. It seems so tiny, so insignificant."

"I tried to call you in LA."

"Did you?"

"Before you left, you said I could come and have a holiday. Don't you remember? I did call you but you were always out. I left my number but you never called back."

"Oh, God, tell me about it. Try finding a maid who speaks English. It's a total nightmare. Do you like my boots? Prada. An absolute fortune but what the hell! I deserve them. Call Nicky. I'm dying to see her."

Carole picks up the phone. "Hi, it's only me. Someone wants to speak to you Nicky."

I take the phone. "Darling. It's me!" I hold the phone away from my ear as Nicky screams.

"Isn't it fab. It's brought back a rush of memories. Especially seeing Carole . . . Yes, you're right (loud laugh). She probably *will* be here in ten years!"

"I'm not playing!" screams Carole. "See I told you! I feel really bloody depressed."

"Come on, Puffin. It's only a game."

"Well, I don't like it. I want to be the successful one."

"I was just getting warmed up." Trust Carole to ruin everything when I was just hitting my stride.

Carole grabs her coat and leaves the restaurant. I go to the cappuccino machine and fill the metal container with milk. Sourpuss is waving at me, but I pretend I don't see her.

The door swings open. Carole marches in.

"Oh, my God!" She stops and forces out a laugh. "You're still here?"

"Wow, you're perceptive!"

"I thought I'd pop in and see Nicky. A play of mine is being performed on Broadway."

"Really? I haven't heard anything about it."

"Maybe you've seen the movie I made with . . ."

I heat up the milk for my cappuccino. The roar of the machine drowns out the rest of Carole's speech.

Carole comes up and shakes my arm.

"You haven't changed," I say. "Still as needy as ever."

She throws down her bag. "It's not fair. You're not playing it properly!"

"I can play it any way I want. No one told you to be all passive. That's your creative choice!"

Carole flings off her coat and goes to the podium. She's crying. "You're horrible."

"Carole, don't be ridiculous! It's only a game."

"Well I don't like it anymore."

"All right. All right." I put my arms around her and kiss her cheek. "We won't play it any more."

"You always say that. Promise we won't."

"I promise."

We both hug. We see that Chicken & Leek Pie is watching us. His book lies closed on the table.

"Do you want the check?" Carole asks him.

He shakes his head. "I love sitting at this table," he says. "It's just like being at the theatre."

Postscript: Shortly after writing this I got a contract to write a best-selling cookbook. My friend Claudia is still a huge success. I'm not sure about old Carole, but she's probably still waiting on tables somewhere.

Chicken & Leek Pie

*L*eeks are synonymous with the Welsh. This dish is one of our big sellers, but some of our customers prefer it with a mashed potato topping instead of pastry. For this, we simply top with mashed potato (see page 93) and bake until the top is slightly browned. Serve with any vegetable such as peas, cauliflower, or broccoli.

SERVES 4–6

PREPARATION TIME: 1 hour and 45 minutes

To prepare the chicken for the filling:
4 large chicken breasts
1 carrot, peeled and chopped
1 stalk celery, chopped
6 peppercorns
2 bay leaves
1/2 onion, peeled and chopped
Salt & pepper

For the filling:
1 cup (2 sticks) butter
1/2 cup flour
2 1/2 cups of the reserved chicken stock
1 1/4 cups milk
1 1/4 cups heavy cream
Salt & pepper
4 large leeks, washed thoroughly and chopped
Chicken, cooked as below

Short Crust Pastry (see page 108)
1 egg, lightly beaten

- To prepare the chicken: Combine all the ingredients in a large saucepan and add enough water to cover the contents of the pan.
- Bring to a boil, then reduce the heat and simmer for 45 minutes to 1 hour, until the chicken is cooked.
- Remove the pan from the heat, strain, and reserve the stock. Discard the vegetables.
- Let the chicken cool a little, then chop it and place it in a deep pie dish to one side.
- Preheat the oven to 350°F.
- Melt 3/4 cup butter in a saucepan over medium heat. Add the flour and cook, stirring constantly, for about 2 minutes.
- Over medium heat, gradually add the chicken stock, then slowly add the milk and heavy cream and stir until smooth. Add salt and pepper to taste.
- In a separate saucepan, sauté the leeks in 4 tablespoons butter until they are nice and soft, then add them to the chicken.
- When the sauce is cooked pour it over the chicken and leeks and stir to combine.
- Cover the dish with the pastry and brush with a little beaten egg. Cut a slit in the top center of the pastry so that the steam can escape while cooking.
- Bake for 35–40 minutes, until the pastry is golden brown.

Steak & Guinness Pie

SERVES 6

PREPARATION TIME: 3 1/2 hours

2 1/2 lbs. steak, cut into 3/4-inch cubes
2 large onions, peeled and chopped
1/4 cup butter
1 tablespoon oil
2 cloves garlic, peeled and crushed
1/2 cup flour
1 tablespoon paprika
1/2 cup brown sugar
4 tablespoons tomato puree
2 1/2 cups Guinness
2 1/2 cups beef stock
2 bay leaves
2 tablespoons dried mixed herbs or 1 bouquet garni
Salt and pepper
Savoury Pastry (see page 110)
1 egg, lightly beaten

♦ Preheat oven to 350°F.
♦ Over high heat, sear the meat in the butter and oil in batches until the meat has been seared and turns brown, about 5 minutes. Remove the meat from the pan and put it to one side.
♦ In the pan juices, cook the onions and garlic over medium heat until soft.
♦ Return the meat to the pan and add the flour, paprika and brown sugar; stir to combine, then add the tomato puree. Cook for 5 minutes over medium heat, making sure the flour has been completely incorporated.

- Add the Guinness and stock, then add the bay leaves and herbs. Simmer very gently, stirring occasionally, for 1 1/2–2 hours. Make sure that the meat is tender before removing it from the heat.
- Add salt and pepper to taste and turn the mixture into a 10-inch pie dish.
- Cover the pie with the savoury pastry and brush it with a little beaten egg.
- Cut a 1/4-inch slit in the middle and bake 35–40 minutes, or until the top is golden brown.

Steak & Kidney Pie

This is another very traditional British dish of which there are also many variations, depending on the part of England the recipe comes from. Some recipes substitute mushrooms for the kidneys, a variation known as John Bull pie, or pudding if you are using suet and steaming it. Steak and oyster pie is also very traditional. I call this the UK-NY version.

SERVES 6

PREPARATION TIME: 3 1/2 hours

1 large onion, peeled and diced
1/4 cup (1/2 stick) butter
2 lbs. beef stew, cut into 3/4-inch cubes
1 lb. veal kidneys
2 tablespoons Worcestershire sauce
1/2 tablespoon English mustard powder
1 teaspoon dark brown sugar
1/2 cup flour
1/2 cup red wine
3 1/2 cups beef stock
Salt and pepper

Savoury Pastry (see page 110)
1 egg, lightly beaten

+ Preheat the oven to 350°F.
+ Over medium heat, sauté the onion in the butter until soft.
+ Add the beef and kidneys and cook, stirring occasionally, for 15 minutes.
+ Add the Worcestershire, mustard, sugar and flour and cook, stirring, for about 5 minutes.
+ Gradually add the red wine, beef stock and salt and pepper to taste and bring to a boil, stirring constantly.
+ Reduce the heat to low and cook for 1 1/2–2 hours, adding a little water if necessary, until the meat is tender.
+ Turn the mixture into a 10-inch pie dish and top with Savoury Pastry. Brush the pastry with a little beaten egg and cut a 1/4-inch slit in the middle.
+ Bake for 35–40 minutes, or until the top is golden brown.

Lamb & Cranberry Pie

The British are famous for their meat pies and have many classic regional recipes for them. This particular one we created ourselves.

SERVES 6
PREPARATION TIME: 3 hours

2 1/2 lbs. boned lamb, cut into 3/4-inch cubes
1/4 cup (1/2 stick) butter
1 tablespoon oil
1 large onion, peeled and chopped
1/2 cup flour

1 teaspoon English mustard powder

Salt and pepper

2 teaspoons Worcestershire sauce

3 1/2 cups beef stock

1/4 cup red wine

1 can whole cranberries

1 Savoury Pastry (page 110)

1 egg, lightly beaten

- Preheat the oven to 350°F.
- Over high heat, sear the lamb in the butter and oil in batches for approximately 5 minutes, until the meat has been seared and turns brown. Remove the lamb from the pan and put to one side.
- To the juices remaining in the pan, add the onions and cook over low heat until soft, then return the lamb to the pan.
- Stir in the flour, mustard powder and salt and pepper to taste and cook, making sure the flour has been mixed in completely, over medium heat, for 5 minutes.
- Gradually add the Worcestershire sauce, beef stock and red wine and bring to a boil. Then reduce the heat to low and simmer for about 1 1/2 hours.
- Add the cranberries during the last 5 minutes of cooking.
- Make sure the meat is tender before removing it from the heat, then add salt and pepper to taste and turn into a 10-inch pie dish.
- Cover the pie with the pastry, brushing it with a little beaten egg.
- Cut a 1/4-inch slit in the middle and bake for 35–40 minutes, or until the top is golden brown.

Spicy Ginger Cake

*T*his cake is very sticky and gooey. I like mine very spicy, so if you prefer it that way, add a little more ginger. It is fantastic with warm custard (see page 94).

2 cups sifted all-purpose flour
1/8 cup ground ginger
1 teaspoon baking powder
1/4 teaspoon salt
4 eggs
1/2 cup (1 stick) butter, softened
1 cup dark brown sugar
1 1/2 cups Tate & Lyle golden syrup
Warm custard, optional (see page 94)

- Preheat the oven to 350°F.
- Butter and flour a 13 1/2 x 4 1/2 x 4-inch loaf pan.
- Mix together the dry ingredients.
- Mix in the eggs, one at a time.
- Add the butter followed by the golden syrup.
- Bake for 40–45 minutes. The cake might sink slightly but will still taste fantastic.
- Serve with warm custard, if you like.

Apple Crumble

This is probably the most commonly eaten pudding in England because it's inexpensive, easy, and quick to put together. I like to add a few blackberries, either canned or fresh, to mine. Instead of apples, you can use 2 cans of drained pitted apricots or plums. The cooking time is more or less the same. I like this with heavy cream poured on top.

SERVES 4–6

PREPARATION TIME: 1 1/2 hours

For the filling:
1 1/2 lbs. Granny Smith or other cooking apples,
    peeled, cored, and sliced
2 tablespoons sugar
5 whole cloves or 1/4 teaspoon cinnamon
1/3 cup water

For the crumble topping:
1/2 cup plus 1 tablespoon sugar
3/4 cup all-purpose flour
1/4 cup plus 1 tablespoon sweet butter
Warm custard or heavy cream, optional (see page 94)

- Preheat the oven to 350°F.
- For the filling, combine the apples, sugar, and spice in an 8 x 8-inch (square or round) buttered baking dish. Add the water.
- For the topping, mix together the sugar and flour and rub in the butter until it resembles bread crumbs.
- Cover the apples evenly with the crumble mixture. Bake, uncovered, for 1–1 1/2 hours, until the topping is golden brown.
- Serve with custard or cream, if you like.

CHAPTER ELEVEN

Pulp Faction

One night, when I arrive at work, Suzy stops chewing on her pen and says quietly, "Table four."

I hang up my coat and look around the restaurant in the natural way one does before a shift. A guy wearing jeans is eating a bowl of chicken soup and looking out of the window. I can't see his face at first, but when he takes another spoonful, I see his jaw rise up. Even I recognize that Punch and Judy profile.

"Quentin Tarantino!" I say. "My God! That's brilliant!"

"I know," Suzy says. "I didn't even see him until I got to the table. I go to put a menu down and the next thing he's looking up at me and asking if I could recommend something. What a week! Julie Andrews yesterday and Quentin bloody Tarantino today!"

I would never have known it was Julie Andrews. This white limo had pulled up outside the restaurant at lunchtime, and in walked two women. One of them had a white hat and sunglasses. They sat at table five and the woman positioned herself so that all you could see was her back.

"It's Julie Andrews!" Suzy whispered before the woman had even opened her mouth.

"How do you know?" As far as I was concerned she was just a wealthy woman with a hat. Suzy gave me a look as if to say "You know me."

Julie Andrews ordered an egg salad sandwich on white bread and a pot of Earl Grey. When she'd finished, Suzy went up with the check and I heard her say "I bet you must wish you had a dollar for every time someone told you this, but the *Sound of Music* is my favorite film."

"Thank you. That's wonderful," replied Julie Andrews in her beautifully clear voice. They then had a bit of a chat and Julie said it was the first proper day off she'd had in two and a half years. After she left, Suzy ran to the deli to buy a phone card and call her Mum with the news.

Suzy has a phenomenal memory for celebrities. She recognizes everyone: musicians, models, fashion designers, presenters, directors—even all the actors on the American daytime soaps. She also has a bizarre knowledge of English soccer players, and what division each team is in, especially Tottenham Hotspur. And she knows the names of every member of the Royal Family and their relationship to each other.

"Can I take Quentin's dessert order?"

"No, you can't!" says Suzy, indignant. "He'll think I don't want to serve him anymore. Anyway, he'll be back."

"Selfish cow," I said. I wanted to see his face close up, to hear him speak, to get a sense of him. There's nothing better than being presented in the raw with a real celebrity, someone you've been looking at for years in magazines or on the screen and suddenly there they are, so familiar, and yet total strangers.

We'd had numerous celebrities over the years, but for me having Quentin in was different: like hardcore LA comes to New York. This was the guy who'd single-handedly liberated a whole generation of filmmakers, a guru who made it cool for thousands of young men to work in video shops while they finished off their screenplays.

In fact it was almost absurd to see the man who had shocked the world with films like *Reservoir Dogs* and *Pulp Fiction* sitting quietly in our little Greenwich Village teashop. The soundtrack of *Sense and Sensibility* was playing for the hundredth time and a smattering of old ladies sat drinking Earl Grey from china cups, carefully spreading clotted cream and strawberry preserves on their scones.

I had to be content to observe him from behind the cake stands. After he finished his soup Suzy persuaded him to have a treacle pudding and custard. She said something to him and he laughed.

One night he was still there, drinking tea, when Carole and I arrived for the night shift. It was a Monday night, so he probably had the night off from the theatre. (I'd found out that he was acting in the Broadway play, "Wait Until Dark." His co-star, Marisa Tomei, was a regular and had recommended us to him.) He sat on table one, beside the podium. The *Village Voice* was spread out in front of him. He circled ads, in pencil, in the real estate section. I was counting out money when he looked up at me as if he wanted to ask a question and then smiled. I blushed and gave him a frozen, self-conscious smile, more like a grimace. He looked quickly down at his paper. Bright red, I carried on counting the money—I was disgusted with myself.

Ever since I'd seen him in here I'd been fantasizing about showing him my film script. When I mentioned it to Carole she gave me a look as if I was mad.

"You can't give him that," she said.

"Why?"

"Why? Because it has no sex, no violence, and no bloody story."

Needless to say, I dropped that idea.

I went to take another table's order. I wished I could be as natural with Quentin as I was with this party of strangers. "Come on," I told myself, "stop being such a prat. He's just another customer."

By the time I looked back to his table, there really was another customer there: A man in his early thirties, wearing a blue plaid shirt and a baseball cap pulled on backward, was sitting in the chair Quentin had just vacated. An attractive blonde woman in her mid-twenties sat opposite. My heart sank. Quentin Tarantino was gone. He might never smile at me again, never get to ask my opinion about the best places to live in Manhattan.

"She's pretty, ya know, blonde, a waspy kind . . ." said the man in the plaid shirt to his companion. His voice was gravelly and loud. Other customers looked up. Carol made a face. "Another noisy American," she muttered.

I look at their check on the hatch: They've ordered two cream teas and Carol is making them a pot of Assam. I put two cups and saucers and a jug of milk on their table. It is obvious they aren't lovers. The girl is sitting erect, with a sort of "I'm paying attention" face. He is slumped over the table, an exercise book open in front of him, the kind kids use for school. Inside, scruffy writing in blue pen is laid out in a script format. I decide that she's an actress and he a writer/director trying to cast a movie.

Next time I pass, the man in plaid is still going strong. "She thinks she's getting the good stuff. She's thinking like, 'OK, this guy is all fucked up, but what do I care?'" The blonde

nods. She picks up her knife and with the other hand feels around for her clotted cream container without taking her eyes off the director.

"Later I'm gonna have her flying outta the window, landing thirty feet below. Everything turns red through the blood. I kinda want drumming going on." He starts to drum on the table, his head nodding in rhythm. "As soon as he whips it out, the drumming stops!" The director gives the table a final bang. There is a dramatic pause before he looks down to his notebook. (I wonder why he doesn't have a computer printout of his script? Even I can do that. Is it cooler to do it long-hand in an exercise book?)

The actress quickly dips her knife into the clotted cream and smears it on the top of her scone, but she's forgotten to slice the scone open. It's going to be difficult to get it all in her mouth, yet still she adds a dollop of jam over the top. She takes a quick bite and instantly wipes her lips with a napkin.

"Jesus, you're stiffing me," he continues. "I love that line! Only my wife could come up with a line like that!"

I move over to Carole, who's making a pot of tea. "Carole, you have to go and listen to that bloke," I say. "It sounds like he's got a worse script than mine."

Sean and Nicky with Rupert Everett. Taken outside the gift shop next door to Tea & Sympathy.

"I can bloody well hear him from here," she replies.

Above the din of the restaraunt comes the name Harvey Weinstein. Then he starts talking big money and dropping names that I've never heard of.

Fortunately, the real celebs don't conform to the stereotypes. Take Rupert Everett. He's been coming in for years and I couldn't say he was one particular way. Sometimes he's very quiet; other times, chatty and full of fun. The only constant is that he's never rude and he tips generously. The problem is that when you encounter celebrities you tend to define them by their behavior at the time you served them, so if they only come in once, your image of them is set.

You can tell when someone wants to be recognized or left alone. Most of the time, it's the latter. The other day Baby Lynsay seated two women on table ten. She thought one of them looked a bit familiar, but didn't really pay her too much attention. The women were very sweet and they left a big tip. Before stepping out of the door, the familiar-looking one turned around and smiled. That was when Baby Lynsay recognized Meryl Streep.

"Fancy sitting Meryl Streep on table ten," I said, put out. She is my favorite actress and the thought of her being hit with an icy blast each time the door opened was upsetting.

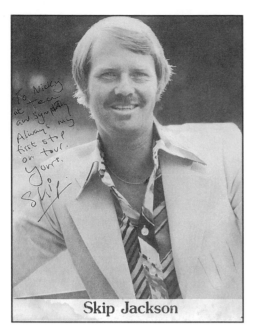

Skip Jackson, a sometime comedian who visits Tea & Sympathy during his infrequent visits to New York, sent us this old publicity shot for our wall of fame.

Skip Jackson

"There were no other tables available," Lynsay wailed. "How was I to know it was her? She was dressed down!"

The director asks me for the check. As I'm adding it up, he tells the girl, "I love this place, I come here all the time."

"It's a really cute place," the girl says. She wraps her untouched scone in a napkin and puts it in her bag.

I give the guy the check. He holds it in front of his eyes while he slides one hand down the back pocket of his jeans. He slumps all the way down his chair and pulls out a couple of crumpled dollar bills. He then stands up and empties a bunch of coins out of his front pockets. He sits down again and counts out nickels and dimes. He stacks them into piles while the girl watches in embarrassment. In between counting he keeps looking back at the check as if he can't remember the amount.

"Just made it," he says.

The last pile, presumably our tip, is the smallest. "Jesus, you're stiffing me," I say to myself.

"Hey, thanks a lot guys," says the movie director. "Everything was great, as usual."

"Thank you. See you again soon," I reply, although I'm not sure I've ever seen him before. I want to tell him that Quentin Tarantino had been sitting in that very chair just before him, but I stop myself—he didn't need to know.

Postscript: Quentin is a regular now. He hadn't been in for a while and Suzy happened to mention to Carole that it was a shame because she really liked him. Carole made some reply to the effect of "Well, it's a shame that he doesn't even know you exist." The last time he was in, before Quentin left he gave Suzy a big hug. "It's great seeing you, Suzy," he said. "I missed you."

Coronation Chicken

This has an Indian flair. We don't make it very spicy in the restaurant, but if I'm making it for myself, I like anything Indian to be quite lively, so feel free to add a little more spice if you wish. This makes terrific sandwiches and may be sliced for finger sandwiches; just add a piece of lettuce before you slice it.

SERVES 6–8

PREPARATION TIME: 2 1/2 hours

3- to 4-lb. whole chicken
1 onion, peeled and chopped
2 tablespoons butter
1/4 cup curry powder
1/4 cup tomato puree
1/2 cup red wine
1 bay leaf
Juice of 1/2 lemon
4 cans of apricot halves, drained of their juice
1/4 cup mango chutney
Salt and pepper
1 cup mayonnaise (see page 141)

- Roast the chicken in a preheated 350°F oven for 1 1/2–2 hours. Cover with foil, so the chicken doesn't dry out, and make sure the pan has been oiled.
- Over medium heat, sauté the onion in the butter. Add the curry powder, tomato puree, red wine, bay leaf, lemon juice, apricots and chutney and simmer until reduced to quite a thick consistency.
- Add salt and pepper to taste. Remove and discard the bay leaf.
- Cool down then stir in the mayonnaise.
- Skin, bone, and chop the chicken. Cool and add to the mayonnaise mixture.

Lancashire Hot Pot

This dish takes its name from the deep brown or white pottery dish that the stew was usually cooked and served in. It is traditionally served with pickled red cabbage. In the restaurant, we serve it with green vegetables.

SERVES 4-6

PREPARATION TIME: 3 hours

2 lbs. boneless lamb, cut into 1-inch cubes
1/4 cup (1/2 stick) butter
3 tablespoons oil
2 onions, peeled and thinly sliced
1/2 cup flour
1 teaspoon Dijon mustard
1 cup red wine
2 tablespoons Worcestershire sauce
1 1/4 cups beef stock
4 large potatoes, peeled and thinly sliced
Salt and pepper

- Preheat the oven to 350°F.
- Sear the lamb in the butter and oil in batches for about 5 minutes, until the meat has been seared and turns brown. Remove meat from the pan and put aside.
- In the juices remaining in the pan, cook the onions until soft.
- Return the meat to the pan with the onions and add the flour, a little at a time, and the mustard.
- Gradually stir in the red wine, Worcestershire and stock.
- Put one third of the lamb mixture into a buttered ovenproof dish, then add a layer

of potatoes, then another layer of meat, and so on, finishing with potatoes. Butter and season the top potatoes.

• Bake for about 1 3/4 hours, or until the potatoes are cooked thoroughly and golden and crispy.

Lamb & Root Vegetable Casserole

Sometimes we make this especially for Rupert Everett because he calls and agonizes if we don't have it. It is deliciously sweet from the vegetables, especially the parsnips, and can be made ahead of time. In fact, it tastes better the next day. Serve this hearty dish in a large bowl with either crusty bread and butter or mashed potatoes on the side.

SERVES 6–8

PREPARATION TIME: 2 hours

2 lbs. boneless lamb, cut into 3/4-inch cubes
1/4 cup (1/2 stick) butter
4 tablespoons oil
2 onions, peeled and diced
2 large leeks, washed thoroughly and chopped
1/2 cup flour
2 tablespoons Worcestershire sauce
2 1/2 cups red wine
2 1/2 cups beef stock
4 carrots, peeled and chopped
3 parsnips, peeled and chopped
3 turnips, peeled and chopped
Salt and pepper

- Sear the lamb in the butter and the oil over high heat in batches for about 5 minutes, until the meat has been seared and turns brown. Remove the meat from the pan and put aside.
- In juices remaining in the pan, sauté the onions and leeks until soft.
- Return the meat to the pan and stir in the flour. Gradually add the Worcestershire, red wine and stock.
- Add the chopped vegetables and salt and pepper to taste and bring to a boil. Boil for a couple of minutes, then reduce the heat and simmer for 45 minutes to 1 hour.

Marmalade/Banana Cake

This is quite a dense sponge cake. If you wish, you can substitute bananas for the marmalade, in which case very ripe bananas are best. If you are making the marmalade version any good marmalade will do, even lemon or ginger. It's best to use marmalade with peel, as it gives it a better texture.

SERVES 10–12
PREPARATION TIME: 2 hours

2 cups sugar
2 cups (4 sticks) butter
9 eggs, beaten
A few drops of pure vanilla extract
4 cups sifted all-purpose flour
2 cups marmalade or 2 ripe
    bananas, mashed

- Preheat the oven to 350°F.
- Grease a 10-inch round cake tin.
- Beat the sugar and butter until light and fluffy.
- Add the eggs, a little at a time, then the vanilla.
- Fold in the flour, then the marmalade or bananas.
- Turn the batter into the prepared tin and bake for 1 1/2–2 hours.

CHAPTER TWELVE

The Spirit
of Christmas

E nough is enough!" shouts Nicky, storming into the restaurant one night with a
piece of paper in her hand. She goes to the sideboard and starts thumping around
in the drawer where she keeps the thumbtacks.

Carole and I exchange smirks above her head. It's nearly Christmas and in between taking orders we've been swigging from a cheap bottle of champagne hidden in the ice tray.
And with a glass or two inside us already, the sight of Nicky on the warpath is quite entertaining.

Nicky rips off an old notice from the Welsh dresser and it flutters to the floor. "Tom
Jones is for night time only," it reads. Underneath, someone has scribbled "Tom Jones sucks."

With Noel and Francisco watching through the kitchen hatch, she pins up her latest staff memo. It's printed up in bold on the new Tea and Sympathy computer:

Hangovers are now banned.
Anyone coming into work hung over will be sent home.
If this occurs a second time they will be fired.
NO EXCEPTIONS.

"Are you going to put it in the menu?" Carole asks. Fortunately, Nicky doesn't hear her, but she turns toward us as she pins a newspaper article underneath the memo. "And this one's for you and Anita," she says, before walking back out of the door. I crane my neck to read the headline: "Drinking and Infertility."

Apparently they've found a link between alcohol and childlessness. I feel a pang of concern: Does drinking really make you infertile? I haven't actually tried having kids yet, but I'm already on the wrong side of thirty-five and the clock is ticking louder by the month. Carole, however, is more concerned with Nicky's latest edict. Our drinking's never been a problem for the restaurant, she says. None of the girls has ever had to go home with a headache.

"It's a bit rich," she moans. "I work fine with a hangover, maybe even better than normal."

The two chefs come out of the kitchen to read the notices. "What is this word?" says Francisco, pointing at the newspaper article.

"Infertility?" I say. "It means, er, 'barren.' You know . . . like if you can't have children."

He thinks for a moment. "Is this why none of you has children?"

"Just because we haven't got a family of four by the time we're twenty," says Carole, rolling her eyes.

"How long you wait? Until you old woman?" Francisco screws up his face and bends over as if he has a walking stick. With his hands he supports an imaginary pregnant tummy.

Noel interrupts. "In Brazil, sometime woman have baby at sixty."

"That's all right then. We'll go and retire to Brazil," says Carole.

"If you want, I give you one child each," Noel says. Carole and I laugh, but the idea shakes me.

I've always fancied Noel. I remember the first day he worked, two years before. I'd just arrived for my night shift and was standing behind the counter having a piece of cake and a cup of coffee when he appeared before me to empty the bus trays. I smiled and introduced myself. He was very shy. That night after work Carole and I spied on him as he changed out of his chef whites into his clothes. He had his back to us but we liked what we saw.

A few days later Noel asked me for a drink: This is what the chefs do because the kitchen is really hot and they get very thirsty. I put on this horrible arrogant voice.

"A drink?" I said. "Can't you see I'm busy? Get back to work and earn your drink, you lazy dog!"

Well of course it all backfired, because even though he only half-understood me, he thought I was serious. He turned red with humiliation and of course I turned red with shame. I tried to tell him I was joking, but he'd disappeared out of sight. Little Jimmy, who was working with him, added fuel to the fire. All night he kept saying things like "You hurt him so much he just try to put his head in the oven." As you can imagine, it rather put the dampers on a flirtation.

Soon Frankie is chatting away in Portuguese (he's from Mexico, but in the kitchen they've all learnt each other's languages). I know he's talking about us, probably telling Noel how Englishwomen don't care for anything except where the next drink is coming from. I remember Pancho once asking me, "But Anita, you never think about tomorrow?"

"Of course I do," I said indignantly. But the truth was, I didn't. Working at Tea & Sympathy was like living in a bubble: It was quite possible to let the years roll by without ever thinking about the future, because every day felt a bit like the future. This was the most pronounced difference between the English waitresses and the South Amer-

Christmas for family and friends at Tea & Sympathy.

ican kitchen staff: They'd come to America because of economics—to save money and build houses in their own countries. They supported children, siblings, and often parents, and those who wanted to remain in America bought cars, saved for houses, and raised families. They had experienced poverty, were grateful for their jobs, and were responsible with their money.

The waitresses were all penniless and unmarried. There were many different reasons why we came, but I think all of us saw New York as a place where anything is possible, where you could spread your wings and fly free. Tea & Sympathy was just the nest from which we'd leap into the jungle beyond. But I'd been working there almost since it opened seven or eight years before and I'd only just begun to peer outside. It's true that quite a few of the waitresses had fallen in love with customers or other staff and had left to get married and have children. But it had always come out of the blue. Nobody seemed more surprised than the girls it happened to. Maybe our psychology had something to do with relying on tips: Earning our money daily made us live from day to day.

Whatever the truth of it, Noel's offer of impregnation had set me off on a new train of thought—and a surprisingly attractive one. For the rest of the night I couldn't stop staring at him. I watched as he prepared the food, his tall slim body framed by the hatch, his olive skin and jet black hair contrasting with his neat chef's whites. There was something calm and refined about his face. His lips were sensuous, and he had a strong masculine jawline straight out of the Harlequin romances I was trying to write in my tiny apartment in the Village. I imagined us lying in bed together in that same apartment while he told me stories of Brazil. Then again, he could hardly speak English, and there wasn't much hope of me mastering Portuguese. So maybe we'd have one of those powerful but silent marriages, where all is understood in a glance, a gesture . . . At that moment Noel looked and caught me staring. He looked embarrassed. I blushed and moved quickly out of sight.

Carole, meanwhile, was still ranting about the new rule. She blamed it on the fast-living English delivery boys next door at Carry On Tea & Sympathy, who wear their hangovers as a badge of courage.

"Of course Nicky's going to get pissed off," she says. "They spend all day moaning about their hangovers. Why don't they keep their mouths shut, or at least pretend they've got food poisoning?"

Through the window I see Sean, with a Christmas tree under his arm and a broad smile, walking across Greenwich Avenue. I feel a sudden thrill. There's only a week to go till Christmas.

When I think of Christmas in New York I'm suffused with the same feelings of pleasure I get from watching an old Woody Allen film. I love the yearly rituals: a trip to see Macy's windows, a free makeover at Bloomingdale's (I've never actually had one but I like to know I can), the lighting of the Christmas tree in Rockefeller Center, and, of course, walking through Central Park on a crisp winter's day to watch the ice-skaters. As the big day approaches I find whatever excuse I can for a trip to the shop next door, where the familiar products transport me back to my childhood. There are tins of Quality Street, boxes of Roses and Black Magic chocolates, bags and bags of Maltesers, and tube upon tube of wine gums. There are Christmas puddings, some with port and others with brandy. There's Christmas cake, Turkish delight, Christmas crackers—and stockings full of every English sweet you can name.

On Christmas Eve we will have our Christmas party. We will close the restaurant early and all traipse into the shop. Sean will organize the music and open bottle after bottle of champagne. Nicky will make a huge saucepan of mulled wine. The kitchen guys will take off their work clothes and dress up for the occasion. It's the only day of the year that all the staff ever get together.

"Come on!" I say to Carole, the Christmas spirit grabbing me. "Let's order a bottle of wine from Manley's."

When Frankie sees the delivery man arrive with our Côtes du Rhone, he claps the side of his head and laughs. But Carole pours him and Noel a glass and the mood changes, as if we're about to have a party. It's not just the wine, but the break in our routine.

Later we order another bottle. Francisco is already drunk and giggly, and Noel, usually so shy, comes out of the kitchen holding his glass. He beckons me over. "Brazilian toast!" he says.

I think he's going on about food until he takes my arm and entwines it with his.

"Oh, a toast!" I say.

The idea is to drink from each other's glass. It's all a bit clumsy because he's taller than I am. His glass bashes against my teeth. Red wine dribbles out of the corner of my mouth. For a second, I think it's blood and my crown has fallen out. I take a noisy slurp and we look into each other's eyes. His are a light brown, the exact same color as the hunting dogs my French uncle always has. As we disentangle, the bare skin of our arms touches and a surge of hot desire courses through my veins. It's a moment of pure Harlequin. And I know that it's love.

Roast Lamb Dinner

I like to serve the lamb with carrots, peas, Brussels sprouts and cauliflower. Don't forget the mint sauce!!

SERVES 6–8

PREPARATION TIME: 2–4 hours, depending on size of lamb

Roast leg of lamb
Baby onions
Roast potatoes
Roast parsnips
Gravy

For the lamb:
5 fresh sprigs rosemary
1/2 cup olive oil
6 cloves garlic, peeled and chopped
Salt and pepper
6- to 7-lb. leg of lamb
1 large onion, peeled and sliced into 1/2-inch rings
4 whole carrots

♦ Lamb Temperature Chart ♦

125°F	Rare
130°F	Medium rare
140°F	Medium—the safe temperature where all harmful bacteria are killed
160°F	Medium well
170°F	Well done

For the baby onions
3 bags of pearl onions

For the gravy:
1–2 tablespoons flour
About 1 1/4 cups meat or vegetable stock
Salt and pepper

- Preheat the oven to 375°F.
- To prepare the lamb: remove rosemary leaves from the stalk and chop coarsely. Combine the olive oil, rosemary, garlic and salt and pepper to taste.
- With a sharp knife, pierce the lamb all over at 1-inch intervals. Shove your finger into each hole as deeply as it will go and stuff the lamb with the rosemary and garlic mixture.
- Cover the bottom of a large roasting pan with the onion rings, then place the lamb on top. Add the whole carrots to the pan and season with a little more salt and pepper.
- Roast the lamb for 20–25 minutes per pound. Check the lamb every 20 minutes for basting.
- To prepare the onions, carefully add the whole onions to a pot of boiling water and blanch them for 1–2 minutes, then drain and plunge them directly into cold water for 1 minute.
- Chop off the end opposite the root and peel off the outer layer.
- Cut a cross in the root end of each onion with a sharp knife.
- When the lamb has 1–1 1/2 hours of cooking time remaining, place the onions around the lamb as they will take 1–1 1/2 hours to cook until they are nice and caramelized.
- After about 1 hour of roasting, insert a thermometer into the deepest part of the lamb. Lamb is supposed to be served slightly pink, not rare. See the temperature chart for your preference.
- While the lamb is cooking, prepare the vegetables.

- When the lamb is cooked, remove it from the oven and let it rest for 15 minutes before carving it, so the juices retreat into the meat.
- This is when you cook all your green vegetables in time for service.

To prepare the gravy: It is difficult to give exact amounts as it depends on the weight of the lamb, but this is a basic method.

- Transfer the cooked baby onions, onion rings, and carrots from the pan onto separate dishes to keep warm.
- Place the roasting pan on the gas or electric ring over high heat to release all of the delicious juices in the pan.
- Add a tiny bit of water and swirl around the pan, scraping the pan with a wooden spoon. Gently transfer the juices to a frying pan and repeat this process until all of the bits stuck to the bottom of the pan are transferred to the frying pan.
- Mash up the carrots and add them to the frying pan along with the onion rings. Bring the mixture to a boil then add 1–2 tablespoons of flour or powdered gravy mix, a little at a time, stirring continuously, and cook for 1–2 minutes.
- Add stock and return to a boil, then reduce the heat and simmer for a minute or two.
- Take a teaspoon of the gravy and let it cool for a minute. Taste to decide whether you need more salt or pepper.
- When it tastes right, remove it from the heat. If you are not ready to serve it straight away, you can reheat at a later time just before serving.

OTHER IDEAS

As an option, you can add a little good red wine to the mixture at the beginning of the process, when the juices first go into the frying pan.

Stuffing

*S*erve with any roast meat, such as the roast lamb on page 187.

SERVES 6–8

PREPARATION TIME: 1 1/2 hours

1 tablespoon butter
1 tablespoon oil
1 large onion (6–8 ozs.) peeled and chopped
4 strips bacon, cut into small pieces
1/2 cup chicken livers, finely chopped
4 pork sausages, cut into small chunks
1 stalk celery, chopped small
1 red apple, cored and finely chopped
Salt and pepper
1 teaspoon dried mixed herbs (herbes de Provence)
1 bunch fresh sage (12–15 leaves), chopped
2 eggs
1/2 cup plain bread crumbs (store-bought bread crumbs are fine)

- Preheat the oven to 375°F.
- Put the oil and butter in a frying pan, enough to coat the bottom of the pan. Sauté the onion until soft and just turning brown.
- Add the bacon, chicken livers, and sausage and cook for 2–3 minutes, until the meat has browned.
- Add the celery, apple, herbs and sage and season with salt and pepper; sauté until everything is cooked and the apples and celery are soft.
- Transfer the mixture to a mixing bowl and add the eggs and bread crumbs; mix well.
- Transfer to an 8 x 8-inch ovenproof dish and bake about 1 hour, until browned and crispy on the top.

Roast Potatoes & Parsnips

SERVES 6–8

For the parsnips:
PREPARATION TIME: 1 hour and 15 minutes

1 or 2 medium parsnips per person
Vegetable oil
Salt and pepper

For the potatoes:
PREPARATION TIME: 1 hour and 40 minutes

Enough to serve 3–4 chunks of potatoes per person
All-purpose flour
Vegetable oil
Salt and pepper

• Preheat the oven to 375°F.
• If large parsnips are the only ones available, you will need to cut out the tough core before slicing the parsnips into finger-sized pieces. Try to make them as even as possible so they will cook evenly.
• Toss the parsnips in good vegetable oil and season with salt and pepper.
• Bake in an ovenproof dish or baking tray, turning them about every 20 minutes to prevent them from drying out and burning, for about 1 hour, or until they are slightly brown and tender. The parsnips will taste much sweeter when they are soft and slightly caramelized, although they are also delicious if you let them crisp up a little, but it's up to you.
• To prepare the potatoes, peel and cut them into the size you would like them. Remember: The smaller they are, the faster they will cook.

- Put the potatoes and 1 teaspoon of salt into a saucepan with enough water to cover them, and bring them to a boil. Boil for 5 minutes, then drain them and pat off any excess water.
- At this point it is nice to roll the potatoes in flour, salt and pepper before coating them with vegetable oil. This is only good when you are roasting the potatoes in the same pan as your roast meat. If you are cooking them separately, you should follow the same procedure as that for the roast parsnips, but the potatoes will take a little longer to cook: Depending on how big they are, they should roast for 1 1/2 hours, or until they are crispy and brown on the outside and soft on the inside.

Epilogue:
The Last Supper

On Christmas Eve, we all get together at Carry On Tea & Sympathy to work on our next hangovers, rules or no rules. It's the first time I've ever seen Noel out of his chef's whites. He offers me a glass of mulled wine and we stand next to each other in silence. We are so close I can feel the heat from his body. Later that night, when the party gets going, we dance. Finally, he pulls me into the office and we kiss.

The next day, everyone's back in Tea & Sympathy proper except for the kitchen staff, who have the day off. Nicky's been cooking for hours. It's the same every year: turkey, special sausage stuffing, roasted parsnips and potatoes, Brussels sprouts, carrots and gravy. The tables are arranged in a semicircle and the restaurant looks like someone's living room. Before long all the waitresses have arrived as well as Nat, Matt, Pat, and Andy, the delivery boys from next door, and most of the family of regulars.

Carole's got a bottle of vodka and is pouring everyone Bloody Marys. Estelle with the bouffon is warming up the crowd with her favorite Cockney songs. Mr. Tooting will probably pass by later. As I arrive, Robert is already there, helping Nicky in the kitchen. When he comes out, Lindsay proudly shows him her Christmas present, a key ring with a picture of her boyfriend's penis. For once, the waitresses are the ones being served and we make the most of it.

But I sit there dreaming of my new Latin lover and our first kiss. In a quiet moment, I lean over to Carole and tell her I'm in love with Noel. She collapses laughing. As it turns out, it's my last Christmas party as a full-fledged Tea & Sympathy employee. Nine months later, give or take a few weeks, Noel and I have our first baby. I was right—it's love.

Another one of Nicky's girls meets and marries a man at Tea & Sympathy. There have been six so far. This is Anita and her husband Noel, the chef.

Photo and Art Credits